BUSINESS FACILITATION

AN ESSENTIAL LEADERSHIP SKILL FOR EMPLOYEE ENGAGEMENT

MIKE PARKES

Matador
9 Priory Business Park
Kibworth Beauchamp
Leicestershire LE8 0RX, UK
Tel: (+44) 116 279 2299
Fax: (+44) 116 279 2277
Email: books@troubador.co.uk
Web: www.troubador.co.uk/matador

ISBN 978 1783062 737

British Library Cataloguing in Publication Data.
A catalogue record for this book is available from the British Library.

Printed and bound in the UK by TJ International, Padstow, Cornwall
Typeset in 12pt Calibri by Troubador Publishing Ltd, Leicester, UK

Matador is an imprint of Troubador Publishing Ltd

This book is dedicated to an old friend and colleague, Chris Hutton, who sadly passed away in August 2013 aged 61.

Chris was an inspiration to me and, having given me my first trainer role back in 1983, influenced and informed my philosophies and thinking on learning and development.

Mike Parkes MCIPD is a founding partner of Momentum Results LLP and former Chief Executive of Development Associates Group Ltd, a subsidiary of Deloitte. A regular presenter on the conference circuit, Mike is the designer and facilitator of the Oxford Retail Masters Forum, at the Said Business School, Oxford University. Mike has over 25 years' experience of advising, guiding and developing leaders working with some of the most prestigious companies across the globe.

www.oxfordsummerschool.co.uk/masters

Foreword

Flick through any organisation's people strategy and I can guarantee that somewhere near the top it will state the following imperative – *to increase employee engagement in order to drive business performance* – yet few have discovered the power of facilitation as a means of achieving this.

That's because the experience most people have of facilitation is when an L&D specialist or external consultant comes in and 'does it to them' ('them' more often than not being senior leaders or a project team of some sorts) but in my experience it's rare for any of those on the receiving end to take it back to their teams. This is either because they lack the confidence to attempt to do what the supposed specialists have 'done' to them or they simply don't see the link with employee engagement.

I first worked with Mike Parkes and his approach to building facilitation skills for leaders about 12 years ago. What appealed to me then, and has continued to remain true since, is that these skills help unlock real engagement and involvement from employees.

This is where this book stands apart for me. It debunks the myth and helps leaders learn practically how to apply the tools and approaches to facilitation in everyday situations. Done well and regularly and soon individuals and teams become accustomed to taking their own decisions, resolving their own problems and initiating their own ideas. Mike and I have worked together many times using these techniques in the organisations I've worked in. Over the course of those learning experiences, I've seen individuals shift a lifetime's engrained perspective of what it is to be a leader. Many learn that being the directive figure of authority whose credibility resides in their ability to take decisions, resolve conflict and control performance was expected and ok at the time, but not going forward.

Whether you're new to leadership or are an experienced old hand, you'll find this book to be a superb resource. I believe you'll gain the insight and motivation to discover what it means to be a leader who can build genuine engagement.

Happy reading and good luck practising the skills of business facilitation.

Mike Hawes
Talent & Capability Director,
Avis Budget Group EMEA

1

Business Facilitation

What is Facilitation?

Facilitation is the art of helping others, in teams, to achieve things for themselves. It grew out of the development of T-groups during the 60's/70's when individuals were brought together for the exploration and development of interpersonal behaviour and were supported in this by a process advisor or facilitator. Its applications have subsequently widened to project groups, management teams and groups on development programmes and have become integral to high engagement.

At times, facilitation is misguidedly regarded as manipulation; facilitators are not the business world's magicians, they don't use slight of hand or tricks of the light. Far from it. Their role is often to help others understand *what* and *how* they are doing things, not conceal their actions or create some form of mystique. Strictly, manipulation is getting the team to do what you want, in the way you want it, when you want it, whilst letting the team believe they chose the route. In reality, facilitation is helping the team decide what they are to achieve, how they want to get there and by when.

What is Business Facilitation?

This is the skill of line managers to engage and encourage their own teams to take greater ownership and responsibility by involving them in decisions that affect them, their business unit or function. This is not seeking their views and then making a decision on their behalf or discussing and debating an issue and when agreement can't be reached taking the casting vote. Instead business facilitation is about ensuring all participants, including the line manager themselves, reach agreement and thereby heighten the level of engagement and performance.

In many ways this can sound rather idealistic; however there are various tools and techniques for achieving this, described throughout this book. Some managers mistakenly believe that business facilitation is about abdicating the responsibility for the outcomes of decisions. Equally, they cannot envisage a scenario where they would actively seek to make decisions with their own team. In truth, not every decision will allow teams to be fully engaged and take ownership for it; some are givens and non-negotiable and the line manager should be explicit about this.

For example, it may have been decided that the function needs to increase sales by 15%, and this is not negotiable, however if how this is achieved is up for grabs, then this provides an opportunity for line managers to business facilitate.

Equally, business vision and strategy is often prescribed from the top of an organisation; however what that means for each function and once again how that is achieved lends itself readily to business facilitation, so encouraging teams to identify workable means for achieving the strategy.

Why has business facilitation developed?

In the past, managers focused and drove employees through direction, control and adherence to strict standards. This may have achieved results in the short term, but this did little to tap into the employees' potential, engage their commitment or engender ownership of the business issues and challenges. With the onset of greater spans of control, increasingly more complex problems and the challenges of the technology age, so managers have sought to create a more empowered workforce. Equally many organisations have seen the direct correlation between an engaged workforce and an increase in business performance.

During 2006-09, B&Q moved their employee engagement scores to achieve the fastest movement by an organisation, in any sector, anywhere in the business world, according to Gallup. B&Q also reported increases in scores in mystery shopping and in March 2007, revealed record business performance. Fraser Longden, Director of HR Retail, attributes this to a core philosophy that a fully engaged workforce will provide outstanding service and in turn deliver the business results. Fraser equally emphasises that this doesn't come easily and that management at every level has to take their responsibilities for employee engagement seriously. At the very core of employee engagement is the manager's ability to business facilitate.

For many managers, business facilitation is often confused with chairing and is seen as a more participative method to manage meetings. In truth, there are a number of fundamental differences between chairing and business facilitation, which are illustrated overleaf.

Chair	Business Facilitator
• Takes responsibility and ownership for achieving the agenda	• Encourages the team to create and own the agenda for themselves
• Drives the meeting to achieve its objectives by instilling energy and decision making practices	• Stimulates the team to raise its own energy levels and agree a means of decision making
• Feels a personal sense of responsibility for the success of the meeting	• Ownership for the success of the meeting rests with the group
• Controls the level of contribution of each participant	• Encourages the group to recognise and manage the interactions of each other
• Manages the interactions of participants and contributes to the debates and decision making process	• Ensures the group decides how they operate and supports them in thinking through and applying their decisions
• Determines when to debate issues, when to make decisions and when to move onto the next issue	• Works at a process rather than content level

For some practitioners, not only is the line between chairing and business facilitating confusing, but questions are often asked as to how facilitation links to *counselling* and *coaching*. Again, although some of the behaviours and skills overlap, there are a number of differences.

Counselling is usually a one to one meeting and is essentially the process of helping individuals to help themselves and is distinguished by the fact that the counsellor is non-directive. In that sense, he or she does not tell the client what to do. Furthermore, the counsellor is non-judgemental by not expressing feelings of approval or disapproval. Although this is true of facilitators, at times it may well be appropriate for the facilitator to be directive with the group.

Coaching equally tends to be a one to one process, however, at times, the coach can be directive, judgemental and fundamentally human as the coach works with the individual to find ways of overcoming a performance difficulty. Furthermore, the conversation can often be initiated by the coach, when they detect a problem; however, the wisest of coaches encourage the individual to take responsibility for not only their problems but also their actions.

Why has business facilitation become integral to Business Effectiveness?

For some time it has been accepted that teams have a higher potential for achievement than individuals working alone. This has been typified by trite phrases such as "1 + 1 = 3" and the concept of 'synergy' banded about at will. Undoubtedly a team's potential is greater than the sum of an individual's solitary contribution. Unfortunately, rarely is this potential fulfilled. All too often the energies, ideas and skills of team members become dissipated and diluted to the lowest common denominator and in fact, individuals working in isolation can often be more effective than in team situations. Fundamentally, effective facilitation supports individuals and teams in identifying and enhancing both their working practices and behaviours such that team and individual goals can be achieved.

Business facilitation's current growth and establishment as an integral skill for both Human Resource Practitioners and Line Managers alike has been attributed to:

- organisations experiencing unprecedented rates of change and needing all individuals to not only respond to both anticipate and precipitate change;

- flatter structures and greater spans of control which have resulted in managers having to manage at a distance, and unable to rely upon dictatorial or controlling behaviours;

- greater autonomy and accountability at lower levels of the hierarchy which has encouraged individuals and teams to question and challenge their working methods and behaviours and take more responsibility for their own effectiveness;

- increased participation and ownership by individuals and teams in determining direction, purpose and performance;

- the increasing expectations of individuals and teams to take ownership and responsibility for their own performance and development.

Business Facilitation has also become integral to managers in a wide variety of sectors. Accountancy and audit has been seen to be a highly mystical process, controlled and policed by financial experts. Annually, auditors would converge on a business to delve into the company's working practices, dissecting each and every activity. Increasingly auditors are attempting to encourage greater ownership and commitment by managers and employees alike to constantly audit their own practices; this is now termed controlled self-assessment. Inevitably this has placed new demands upon the auditors and our work in this field has shown that equipping auditors with the skills to business facilitate can encourage line managers to create their own very effective regulatory practices. Despite many concerns that this approach would result in the auditors' role becoming redundant, surprisingly it has made their role more challenging and of greater value, as much of the menial and laborious work is attended to locally. Instead, they are able to focus their skills and energies on priority areas as well as working at more strategic levels.

Business Facilitation has also grown within the IT profession as IT specialists seek to engender the commitment of various interested parties to the installation of new systems or networks. Traditionally, this has been approached from a heavily expert based perspective, so when faced by resistance, the IT specialist has had to resort to supplying more and more data and rational arguments to win over others' support. This has clearly been somewhat of a chaotic process and many have turned to facilitation to support them in handling the differing agendas, experiences and perspectives of the various parties.

Finally, even in the field of medicine and healthcare, there have been a number of fundamental shifts as doctors and pharmacists alike seek to reduce the dependency upon them. This is not to suggest that they are taking less responsibility, but more that this becomes shared with the patient so that rather than constantly prescribing medicines to deal with the symptoms of illness, practitioners are seeking to educate patients on preventative health care which is more likely to attend to the root causes.

What Philosophies Underpin Business Facilitation?

1. The more that teams and individuals come to their own conclusions, the greater the likelihood that they will be committed to effecting change.

    Fundamentally, individuals tend not to like being directed. There is the tendency to believe that our own ideas are often the best and many of us are determined to make these work despite the problems and barriers we face. This principle is imperative in encouraging individuals and teams to take responsibility for their own direction. In other words, waiting for others to take the lead might encourage feelings of comfort; in reality it serves to create powerlessness in oneself and fundamentally inhibits growth and development.

2. All teams and individuals have the potential to increase their effectiveness.

   Often, teams and individuals are classed as effective or ineffective. In reality this is a fallacy. All groups and individuals are unique – all have their own different characteristics and as a result, cannot be compared. I can remember in my formative days in management, observing a colleague struggle and battle to achieve small amounts of success, yet receive constant praise and recognition, whereas another colleague coasted to success whilst receiving very little encouragement. I thought this strange until I began to understand that the first colleague had sought to stretch and challenge themselves to their limits to achieve small wins whilst the second colleague had made very little effort and hardly exerted themselves and was therefore performing substantially short of their true potential.

   Thus, regardless of the individuals' comparative performances, there is always scope for improvement. The brilliant can become super-brilliant or even exceptionally brilliant; the ineffective can become less ineffective. In essence the label placed on the team or individual is in many ways irrelevant, there is always scope for improvement. The role of the business facilitator is to help the team achieve the next stage in their progression, rather than becoming complacent.

3. Teams and individuals should be helped in their working practices in such a way as they continue to succeed long after the manager has gone.

   Some managers glory in their role, drawing attention to their wealth of experience and expertise, and become destined to share this whether the team deems it important or not. They can become preoccupied with their own self importance and unfortunately for teams, the net effect is that they become dependent upon the manager. More to the point, they value this dependency because hard work and thinking is removed from them and life is made much easier. The manager will create a dependency culture, unless they begin to let go and provide opportunities for the team to take wider responsibility.

4. The way in which individuals and teams work provides a valuable vehicle for learning.

For many teams, individuals and business facilitators, there is the common misconception that learning is synonymous with problems and difficulties. More so, the greater the difficulty so the likelihood of learning increases. In reality, such scenarios may highlight the learning opportunities more readily; however, the workplace provides a wealth of daily learning experiences. In truth, learning should be synonymous with reinforcing positive behaviours and recognising and overcoming negative behaviour. As much can be learned from a success as from a failure, as the good practices and behaviours are distilled and reinforced and learning becomes a positive and enjoyable experience and not an inquiry into what went wrong. Furthermore, groups become so obsessed with the task in hand that the process and the way in which they are working become neglected. It is only at moments of crisis that thought is given to how we have reached this position. Every situation has immense learning opportunities. The challenge is whether groups are committed to capitalising upon these; do they want to learn from success or only from failure?

How does business facilitation differ from traditional learning facilitation?

	Business Facilitator	Learning Facilitator
Purpose/ Objectives	Either set by the business facilitator or jointly with the team.	Set and agreed by the participants themselves in conjunction with the facilitator.
Exploration of Issues	Will provide frameworks for drawing out the issues, but will also be involved in the discussions and debate.	Will tend to be removed from the discussion, intervening to deal with issues about the way in which the team is working or learning.
Generation of Ideas	Will encourage the team to generate ideas, may add their own but will minimise the amount of their contribution.	Ensures the team generate ideas without adding their own.
Agreement and Decisions	Jointly agreed by all, using methods, usually suggested by the business facilitator.	Agreed by the group, with the facilitator providing methods to achieve this.

Key Terminology

Throughout the book, a number of facilitation terms are regularly used and these are often the source of much confusion and debate, therefore, definitions are provided below to help explain how the words are applied in this book.

Challenge	The process of encouraging individuals to examine issues in a different light.
Climate	The ambience or atmosphere of the team which is determined by their common behaviours and working practices.
Confront	The process of presenting an individual/team with their behaviour, thereby enabling them to make decisions about how they operate in the future.
Content	The topic being discussed.
Empower	The process by which individuals take responsibility for themselves, their behaviours and actions.
Feedback	The giving of non-judgemental information about the effect that an individual's behaviour has had on you.
Intervention	A statement, question or action by a facilitator to raise an issue with an individual or group for them to consider and address.
Norms	The team's established ways of behaving and working.
Personalise	Individuals talking about themselves rather than people in general.
Process	The ways in which individuals and teams interact and work together.
Review	The method by which a team reflects and considers their actions and plans for improvement.

2

The Skills of Business Facilitation

Mystique surrounds the skills of business facilitation. At times it requires very active involvement; on other occasions more observation and reflection. Fundamentally the over-riding purpose of the manager of any team is to ensure that the team achieves results through the ownership and accountability of the team members. For many practitioners, capturing and analysing the skills of business facilitation is a challenge in itself. In working in a field which is an art not a science, many attempts have been made to categorise business facilitation behaviour. However, the true challenge is not the categorisation but the application; what makes it right to provide direction in one scenario, but less appropriate in another, or knowing when to or not to become involved relies on the skill and judgement of the business facilitator.

The skills of business facilitation are by no means unique to this role. Observation, listening, questioning and confronting are common to most managerial roles. However, underlying every form of business facilitation is the desire for ownership and problem resolution to remain within the team. As previously mentioned, but worth emphasising, business facilitation is only effective when the manager wants the team to make and own certain decisions. If the issue and decision is not open to debate, then traditional management approaches are more relevant, i.e. directing, re-affirming, and explaining.

This chapter examines the skills and styles of the business facilitator, in addition to examining the appropriate application of these skills.

In 1990, spurred on by the endless clarifications, none of which seemed to reflect my own experiences of facilitation, I sought to create a new classification which I felt reflected my own day to day facilitator behaviour.

For a period of eighteen months, following every intervention I made, I wrote down what I said and why. Initially, this seemed like an endless list of different interventions for different reasons, but having sat down and examined the plethora of options, the outcomes were somewhat amazing. The vast array of interventions were in fact often variations on a theme and the facilitator behaviour could simply be defined. This experience is now encapsulated in the following intervention model.

Intervention Model

Intervention is the act of involving oneself with a group by asking questions, providing information, expressing feelings or otherwise altering the course of action that is being taken. This model has been developed from the practical experiences of facilitators working with a wide range of groups with differing needs and purposes.

Stage 1 : Data Gathering/Problem Analysis

In any group, the facilitator will need to make decisions about the most appropriate intervention. This stage is the basis from which those judgements are made.

There are four key considerations in gathering data:

(i) Direction
- What is the group trying to achieve?
- In what direction should they be going?
- What is their desired outcome
- What would success feel like?

(ii) Content
- What is actually being said?

(iii) Process
- How is it being said and to whom?
- What is the tone of the statement, the body language which supports it, the message which seems to be coming across etc?

(iv) Relevance
- How does what's being said help the group to achieve their objective?
- How does it help the process?

Armed with this data, the facilitator can then select the intervention which he/she feels is most appropriate.

Stage 2 : Intervention Style

Once the facilitator has gathered enough data to confirm that an intervention is necessary in order to move the group on, the next decision is "what intervention will be most effective?" There are ranges of different interventions that can be used:

Directive   This intervention provides the group with ideas or suggestions for moving forward.

Example	"Because of the difficulties you have expressed, I would suggest you review the way in which you are working."
	"Groups often find it difficult to come up with ideas in this area. I would suggest that you try brainstorming."
Questioning	As the name suggests, this style of intervention encapsulates the wide range of different questions that may be asked. This not only includes the traditional open and closed questions, but also includes clarifying questions.
Example	"So are you saying that you are unclear about what's being asked of you?"
Observation	This style of intervention utilises the business facilitator's observations to express either what he/she sees happening or how he/she feels about what is happening.
Example	"I have noticed that before we have reached agreement on one issue, we move onto the next issue."

The intervention styles are not mutually exclusive. In fact, they are often used in combination with each other:

Example	"A number of you seem uncertain, I would suggest we discuss this." *(Observation Directive Intervention).*

Stage 3 : Focus for Intervention

This is the stage at which you decide who to direct the intervention at;

this can be with an individual, a sub-group (a number of individuals) or the entire group.

Stage 4 : Application and Review

This is quite simply applying the chosen intervention and reviewing its effectiveness, which then leads the facilitator back into Stage 1.

Intervention Model

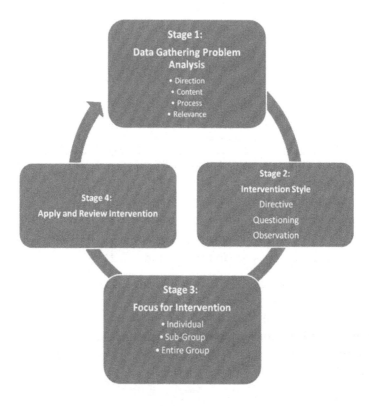

Intervention Questionnaire

Situation	Intervention	Intervention Type?	Focus?
1. A group is working to prepare a presentation. When you go along to check on progress they have not moved ahead and are struggling to get organised.	A. "Perhaps if you split into smaller groups and took a part of the presentation each you will get on better." B. "I am very concerned that you don't seem to have made any progress as yet."		
2. One member of the group has not made any contribution to the session.	A. "How effectively do you think you are involving everybody so far?" B. "Mary, what are your views on the session so far?"		
3. The group is struggling to grasp the meaning of the written brief you have given them.	A. "Would you like me to clarify the brief?" B. "John seems to have understood the brief. Perhaps he could be of help to the rest of you."		
4. During a team exercise one member has taken control. The others are clearly displeased but have not said anything.	A. "Jan, how would you describe your role in the team right now?" B. "I can see that several of you are looking uncomfortable at the moment. What can be done about that?"		

Situation	Intervention	Intervention Type?	Focus?
5. One member of the group persists in focusing attention onto a personal problem that he has. This is blocking the group from making progress.	A. "Alan, what impact do you think you are having on the group?" B. "Alan is clearly concerned about this problem. How would you suggest that you can move forward with the session but ensure that you meet Alan's needs?"		
6. Several times the group has strayed from the main issue and started to gossip about the business.	A. "There seems to be some problem in focusing on the issues. How would you suggest that your discussions might become more focused?" B. "This issue does not seem relevant. Mary, can you remind the group of the objective of this session."		
7. During the introduction session some members of the group are unclear about the programme objectives and don't know why they are here.	A. "Perhaps those of you who have been briefed would tell the group what your understanding of the objectives is." B. "I appreciate and understand the confusion in the group. Would it help if we discuss the objectives now to clear up any misunderstandings?"		

Situation	Intervention	Intervention Type?	Focus?
8. In the middle of an exercise there is some conflict in the group and one member bursts into tears and runs out of the room.	A. "Jenny might I suggest you check on Jane." B. "I am worried that Jane is upset. However, I think it is important that you decide how best to handle the situation. What ideas do you have?"		
9. The group has been working hard to help a member to see the opportunities which exist to improve an interpersonal problem at work, but he is rejecting all of their ideas.	A. "John, your response leaves me confused as to whether or not you want to resolve this issue." B. "Perhaps you could move on to someone else and return to John when he seems more receptive."		
10. The group is having difficulty generating ideas to get started on a problem.	A. "Why don't you each take 2 minutes and write down as many ideas as you can and then discuss them one by one?" B. "You seem to be stuck at the moment. What ways could you think of to generate some ideas?"		
11. A member of the group asks another a personal question. In respond the questioner is told to "mind his own bloody business" and an argument ensues.	A. "Ian, what was your motive for asking that question?" B. "Jane, you seemed to react defensively to Ian's question. Could you explain why?"		

Situation	Intervention	Intervention Type?	Focus?
12. There is a confidentiality issue amongst the group which is stopping some members from contributing.	A. "I am aware that some of you are looking uncomfortable and are holding back. What would need to happen to help you to be more open with the group?" B. "Perhaps we could move ahead by setting some ground rules about confidentiality, which we can all agree to and stick by."		

Intervention Questionnaire – Answers

Situation	Intervention	Intervention Type?	Focus?
1. A group is working to prepare a presentation. When you go along to check on progress they have not moved ahead and are struggling to get organised.	A. "Perhaps if you split into smaller groups and took a part of the presentation each you will get on better." B. "I am very concerned that you don't seem to have made any progress as yet."	A. Directive B. Observation	A. Group B. Group
2. One member of the group has not made any contribution to the session.	A. "How effectively do you think you are involving everybody so far?" B. "Mary, what are your views on the session so far?"	A. Questioning B. Questioning	A. Group B. Individual
3. The group is struggling to grasp the meaning of the written brief you have given them.	A. "Would you like me to clarify the brief?" B. "John seems to have understood the brief. Perhaps he could be of help to the rest of you."	A. Directive (an implied suggestion within the question) B. Observation and Directive	A. Group B. Group (John is included)
4. During a team exercise one member has taken control. The others are clearly displeased but have not said anything.	A. "Jan, how would you describe your role in the team right now?" B. "I can see that several of you are looking uncomfortable at the moment. What can be done about that?"	A. Questioning B. Observation and Questioning	A. Individual B. Group or sub-group (if the facilitator indicates non verbally who the individuals in question are.

Situation	Intervention	Intervention Type?	Focus?
5. One member of the group persists in focusing attention onto a personal problem that he has. This is blocking the group from making progress.	A. "Alan, what impact do you think you are having on the group?" B. "Alan is clearly concerned about this problem. How would you suggest that you can move forward with the session but ensure that you meet Alan's needs?"	A. Questioning B. Questioning and Directive	A. Individual B. Sub-group (all except Alan)
6. Several times the group has strayed from the main issue and started to gossip about the business.	A. "There seems to be some problem in focusing on the issues. How would you suggest that your discussions might become more focused?" B. "This issue does not seem relevant. Mary, can you remind the group of the objective of this session."	A. Observation and Questioning B. Observation and Directive	A. Group B. Individual
7. During the introduction session some members of the group are unclear about the programme objectives and don't know why they are here.	A. "Perhaps those of you who have been briefed would tell the group what your understanding of the objectives is." B. "I appreciate and understand the confusion in the group. Would it help if we discuss the objectives now to clear up any misunderstandings?"	A. Directive B. Observation; Directive and Questioning	A. Sub-group B. Group

Situation	Intervention	Intervention Type?	Focus?
8. In the middle of an exercise there is some conflict in the group and one member bursts into tears and runs out of the room.	A. "Jenny might I suggest you check on Jane." B. "I am worried that Jane is upset. However, I think it is important that you decide how best to handle the situation. What ideas do you have?"	A. Directive B. Observation, Directive and Questioning	
9. The group has been working hard to help a member to see the opportunities which exist to improve an interpersonal problem at work, but he is rejecting all of their ideas.	A. "John, your response leaves me confused as to whether or not you want to resolve this issue." B. "Perhaps you could move on to someone else and return to John when he seems more receptive."	A. Observation B. Directive and Feelings	
10. The group is having difficulty generating ideas to get started on a problem.	A. "Why don't you each take 2 minutes and write down as many ideas as you can and then discuss them one by one?" B. "You seem to be stuck at the moment. What ways could you think of to generate some ideas?"	A. Directive (an implied suggestion within a question) B. Observation and Questioning	A. Group B. Group
11. A member of the group asks another a personal question. In respond the questioner is told to "mind his own bloody business" and an argument ensues.	A. "Ian, what was your motive for asking that question?" B. "Jane, you seemed to react defensively to Ian's question. Could you explain why?"	A. Questioning B. Observation and Questioning	A. Individual B. Individual

Situation	Intervention	Intervention Type?	Focus?
12. There is a confidentiality issue amongst the group which is stopping some members from contributing.	A. "I am aware that some of you are looking uncomfortable and are holding back. What would need to happen to help you to be more open with the group?" B. "Perhaps we could move ahead by setting some ground rules about confidentiality, which we can all agree to and stick by."	A. Observation, Questioning and possibly Directive (implications are that they should be more open) B. Directive	A. Group or Sub-group (if the facilitator indicates non-verbally who the individuals are) B. Group

Observation Skills

The data gathering/problem analysis stage of the intervention model is in essence a test of the business facilitator's ability to share and analyse team behaviour.

In all major interactions there are three key elements; the task, the content and the process. In focusing upon the task, the facilitator is concerned with what is being achieved. In examining the content, the business facilitator is concerned with the subject matter, whilst focusing upon the process, and the way in which the group is working together. All too often, business facilitators find themselves jumping between these three different aspects only to find themselves lost and confused.

The skill of observation is to establish *what's* being achieved and *how* it's being achieved. The most significant areas to observe are listed below.

What to look for:

Objectives	Does the group have clear objectives? Are their behaviours and actions supporting the achievement of the objectives?
Strategy	Have the group articulated and agreed their plan and strategy? Have the group agreed their working practices?
Groundrules	Have the group agreed their groundrules for working together? To what extent are they working to these?

Decision Making   What is their decision making process?
To what extent is this dominated by the few?
What problems are they experiencing in making decisions?

Individual Styles   What is the predominant behaviour of each individual?
How influential is each individual?
To what extent is each individual's contribution valued?
To what extent do individuals show signs of holding back?

Team Interaction   What is the level of participation?
To what extent do the group go off on tangents?
Are there any signs of sub-groups or cliques?
Who talks to whom?
Do the group build upon each other's ideas?
To what extent do they interrupt/ignore each other's contributions?
What is the quality of listening taking place?
To what extent does the group engage in positive or negative feedback with each other?
Do group members readily reveal their views, opinions and feelings?
To what extent do group members encourage contributions from each other?

Team Climate   To what extent is there a climate of openness/honesty?

Do the group use humour to cover up difficulties?
To what extent are conflicts and disagreements
worked through?
Is the climate one of politeness and passivity or is
there challenge, rigour and willingness to confront
issues?
What is the level of energy within the group?
Is the climate one of real commitment and
satisfaction?

Body Language What messages are members of the group's body
language conveying?
To what extent do any of the non-verbal signals
seem to contradict what is being said?
Are there any non-verbal signals which suggest
there are hidden issues?

How Do You Observe?

Faced by the wide range of team processes and dynamics, facilitators can become obsessed with attempting to capture every single interaction and as a result, become so absorbed in the data collection phase they become paralysed to intervene.

Observation requires the business facilitator to become quick at recognising the nature of interactions rather than quick at capturing everything that happens. In aiding this process, there are a number of guidelines for facilitators:

i) Find the trends

Rather than attempting to capture every minute detail, seek the trends and attempt to establish the recurring themes. Teams can often recite back what happened and when, but they are often too closely involved to recognise the behavioural issues which keep recurring.

For example, the fact that an individual interrupts a colleague in itself may be of little significance; but if there is a constant pattern with interruptions resulting in the loss of ideas, this may be an issue for the team to attend to.

ii) Recognise your own assumptions

When business facilitating, we often bring with us our own bias and prejudices around individual and team behaviours and can at times jump to conclusions. For example, when working with a team, we might notice that one individual has been quiet for some time. We might also notice that the individual is not making eye contact with the rest of the team and from this, we might jump to the conclusion that they are confused or uncomfortable or have even opted out. However, in reality, the only thing we can be sure of is that they have not said anything, nor have they made eye contact with the rest of the group. Thus rather than making a sweeping statement "Phil, you're not involved", thereby potentially inflaming the situation, the opportunity exists to ask a question, "what were you thinking?"

Equally an individual who says exactly what's on their mind in a very direct manner, may be described by some as confident, by others as honest, by a number as arrogant. In truth the same behaviour can be interpreted very differently depending upon our own bias and prejudice.

iii) Be broad and detailed

As discussed earlier, many business facilitators become obsessed with the detail, whilst others rely solely on observing at the broad level. Each can be equally limiting. The dilemmas with poorly detailed observations have already been described; however, purely operating at the broad level may mean that examples to support the trends you have identified may be lost. These examples can be invaluable to teams both in recognising their behaviour and processes and in indicating how they might change.

iv) Observe the content, the task and the process

Many managers new to business facilitation can find themselves drawn into examining the content of discussions, as individuals begin to describe their thoughts and ideas. Internally, the manager begins evaluating what the individual has said, deciding whether they agree or have an alternative view. As the managers progress with their skills of business facilitation, many begin to recognise the importance of observing team processes and some would argue that the role of the business facilitator is to focus as much upon the process as on the content of what is said. In fact for many years, I supported this notion and would often profess that one does not need to understand the content in order to facilitate the process. Unfortunately, I learned the importance of having to observe and listen to both when attempting to facilitate the development of teams working within the nuclear power industry.

The quality of teamwork is fundamental to the management of the power station's control room. Having been invited to support the control room's development of teamworking, I found myself observing groups who would talk to each other by referring to various elements of equipment, numbers and systems, in a room that looked like Star Treks "Enterprise". I had no way of detecting whether what one person said to another had any relevance, or whether their working practices and group processes were supporting their fulfilment of objectives.

v) Avoid self-fulfilling prophecies

At times we can quickly recognise the behaviours present in the group. However, armed with this data, the challenge facing us as facilitators is not to keep looking for evidence to support this notion. Often the more we look for something, the more we are likely to spot supporting evidence; however, the less likely we are to spot evidence which counters this view. In effect, by spotting issues too early we can create self-fulfilling prophecies. The challenge to us as facilitators is to actively seek data which counters our initial view, only by the absence of this and further examples of supporting data can we be sure of our conclusions.

vi) Be mindful of our own hobby-horses

As human beings, it can be a challenge for all of us to remain wholly objective throughout. Certain comments, behaviours and traits can be distracting for each one of us. For example, we may have certain aversions to very aggressive and dominant behaviour and therefore are very quick to recognise this in its many forms, but unfortunately this may be to the exclusion of recognising other more subtle behaviours taking place.

By contrast, some facilitators focus more upon those who are speaking, whilst others observe the reactions to what is being said, or the whole group process. In reality, all of these elements are important and a preoccupation with any facet can limit the quality of the facilitator's observations.

Where Do You Observe From?

Facilitators constantly face the dilemma of deciding where do they position themselves physically. How do they see the whole group, and yet be unobtrusive? How do they sit within the group without feeling compelled to join or become a source of distraction?

In reality, different facilitators have different personal preferences and this variety is also mirrored by group preferences. What is important is the recognition of the strengths and limitations of different vantage points and the facilitator's willingness to be flexible in positioning themselves.

Positioning within the group

Strengths

- You can see all group members and therefore have a greater possibility of picking up on the body language.

- It is less difficult to intervene, in that your voice comes from within the group rather than from afar.

- It allows you to detect individuals' reactions to your intervention.

- It is potentially easier to build a relationship with the group in that they are not looking over their shoulders wondering what is going on.

Limitations

You can feel compelled to join in.

- Any prolonged periods of silence on your part can serve to unsettle individuals as they become preoccupied with what you are thinking, rather than what they should be doing or see you as a group member and expect you to behave as such.

- Your departure can be disruptive and individuals can become intrigued as to what has happened and why you left.

- The fact that you can observe the entire group, can work in reverse. **They** can see **you** and therefore may seek to detect any non-verbal reactions on your part to their discussions. This can serve to influence groups, particularly in the early stages of their development as they often seek affirmation for their decisions.

Positioning outside of the group

Strengths

- Unobtrusive, in that you are not easily a source of distraction and therefore it allows you the freedom to decide how much or little you may wish to intervene.

- It is easier to come and go from the room.

- Standing back from the group can make it easier to detect the main themes, despite not necessarily being able to detect all the non-verbal behaviours taking place.

- It sends a clear message that you are not part of the group and the responsibility rests with them.

Limitations

- It can make the group feel like 'big brother' is watching them.

- It can feel awkward to intervene.

- Any intervention you make naturally draws attention and possibly responsibility from the group and thus it does not necessarily become part of the group's conversation. By contrast, interventions made whilst positioned within the group have a greater likelihood of merging into the discussions.

Moving between these two positions

Strengths

- It provides you with flexibility in the role that you play.

- It allows you to combine the strengths of both positioning in and out during an entire session.

- Providing that you are clear that you are likely to become heavily involved, ie as a group moves into a review process, this can signal your support.

Limitations

- There is the danger that you become a 'jack-in-the-box', moving from one to the other and therefore a severe distraction.

- It is often difficult to know whether you will need to move into the group for a prolonged period as you might initially move in and then realise that you are not really required and then become stuck.

- Groups can become preoccupied with the fact that you have moved in or moved out.

Moving in and out of the room

Strengths

- Continual observation is a draining process and periods out of the group can re-energise the sharpness of the facilitator's observation skills.

- It can be easier to detect differences in the group processes by contrasting current behaviour with your previous experiences of that group.

- Moving around groups provides facilitators with the opportunity to share observations and therefore enhance their own skills as well as increasing the accuracy and breadth of what has been seen.

Limitations

- Clearly, issues will be missed, although if one is truly concerned with the trends, then if the issues are significant there is the likelihood that they will occur again.

- Again, the movement can be distracting for the group and a source of discussion.

- The facilitators move so readily between eachgroup that they have scant data on any group.

Notetaking

Finally a few words on capturing your observations:

If you are positioned within the Group

- Avoid taking notes. Groups will become preoccupied in speculating what is being written down.

- Attempt to memorise the key trends and make any necessary notes once you have left the group.

If you are positioned outside of the Group

- It can be easier to take notes, but do not undertake excessive notetaking as the group will begin to notice them and again will serve to distract.

Applying the Intervention

Having positioned yourself, observed the group, diagnosed the issues, selected your intervention, all that is left is the mere art of applying your intervention.

As the model has shown, this stage is concerned with applying a directive, questioning, feeling (or combination) intervention. However, this is the first phase that demands interaction within the group. Until this juncture, your entire energy has been channelled into seeing and thinking. Now you have moved to that delicate phase of doing, when all our observations, thoughts, hypotheses are rigorously tested and facilitation moves from a cerebral to dynamic activity with all the complications that groups bring.

The success of the intervention will largely depend upon three key factors:

1. The degree to which the intervention is meaningful and necessarily relevant to the group.

2. The tone that is being used.

3. The words that are used.

1. The degree to which the intervention is meaningful and necessarily relevant to the group

There is greater likelihood of the group accepting the intervention if they can readily understand not only what is being said, but that they can also see its direct relevance to what is happening, how they are operating or where they are going. All too often, facilitators make interventions which are too oblique or subtle. Unfortunately, groups involved in the humdrum of group activity, find it difficult to move their thinking from one avenue to another (for example, content to process) without some form of indication that this is happening.

An example:

Asking a high energy group who are all contributing ideas and participating fully, "What has just happened?" is unlikely to result in the fullest description possible. The individuals are likely to be so absorbed with generating and analysing ideas that they are unlikely to be aware of what has just happened. They may need more help in recognising what has taken place, for example "There are a lot of ideas being generated at the moment. Just stop for a moment and think about how we are handling this."

Alternatively, the facilitator may chose to articulate the observations they have made through a "feelings" intervention. For example, "There seem to be a lot of ideas being generated. One of the things I've noticed is that some of these are being written on the flipchart whilst others are not, without any apparent discussion".

2. The tone that is being used

The tone that a facilitator uses can not only determine how palatable the intervention is, but also influence its impact.

A very firm or even aggressive tone can encourage the group to become defensive, despite how meaningful or relevant the words are. This defensiveness may well result in the intervention being rejected. Equally, a very quiet, soft tone can often be overlooked in a very robust group and thus often requires persistence and resilience to sustain the intervention and force the group to confront the issues being raised. The impact of the tone related to the highly energetic and vocal groups is summarised in the model below.

In the context of this model, high tone means loud, forceful and enthusiasm, whilst low tone means softer, quieter, providing more resistance.

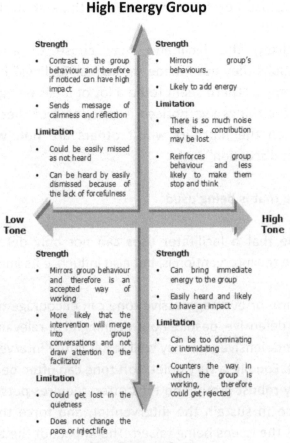

High Energy Group

Strength

- Contrast to the group behaviour and therefore if noticed can have high impact

- Sends message of calmness and reflection

Limitation

- Could be easily missed as not heard

- Can be heard by easily dismissed because of the lack of forcefulness

Strength

- Mirrors group's behaviours.

- Likely to add energy

Limitation

- There is so much noise that the contribution may be lost

- Reinforces group behaviour and less likely to make them stop and think

Low Tone

High Tone

Strength

- Mirrors group behaviour and therefore is an accepted way of working

- More likely that the intervention will merge into group conversations and not draw attention to the facilitator

Limitation

- Could get lost in the quietness

- Does not change the pace or inject life

Strength

- Can bring immediate energy to the group

- Easily heard and likely to have an impact

Limitation

- Can be too dominating or intimidating

- Counters the way in which the group is working, therefore could get rejected

Low Energy Group

3. The words that are used

The degree to which the intervention is relevant and meaningful can be high and the time can be appropriate. However, the intervention often fails because of the words used. It is not necessarily the case that the words are meaningless or applied incorrectly in the context of the dictionary, more that they conjure up reactions which are not anticipated. For example, some words create a natural inclination for individuals and groups to become defensive, whilst others' words become an instant turnoff to the recipients. Although the individuals' words may be acceptable in isolation, it is the essence of the statements which conjure up the various group reactions.

These statements can be grouped into two types:

Judgemental

Those words, phrases or statements in which the group feel that they have been judged, reprimanded or addressed in a punitive manner. These statements often contain the words 'you', 'should', 'right', 'wrong'.

Eg: "You don't seem to have done this task very well"
    "I've seen other groups do this much quicker"

In both of these instances, the group is likely to become defensive, regardless of the accuracy of the statement.

Training Mode

Those words, phrases or statements which sound as if they are coming from a training manual and therefore can seem trite or manufactured. Although the words and phrases may be highly appropriate, their overuse has resulted in their impact being devalued. In fact, for many of us, they are the phrases that make us cringe, whilst they are likely to bring jocular responses from group members.

Eg: "How do you feel about that comment?"
    "Are you comfortable with that?"

The words 'feeling' and 'comfortable' tend to impact on pragmatic line managers as 'touchy/feely' and as a result, somewhat distant from the rugged day to day challenges they face. The sentiment of the sentences themselves may be wholly appropriate, but these two words have undermined its impact. This is not to say that feelings are not important. Far from it. They are essential at unearthing group dynamics, processes and working practices, but the phrases need to be palatable to the audience. It is likely that asking the individual what their reaction is would generate the same data. What do they think of what has just been said? Or what is going on? This is not to say never ask about feelings, simply be mindful of the audience and the degree to which the words are used.

Finally, the word 'comfortable' rarely deals with the issue at hand. I may be comfortable with an idea, meaning I understand it, but resent the notion intently. Furthermore, the concept of comfortable tends to be associated with being physically relaxed, content and easy, not whether you agree or disagree with something.

Stereotypical Business Facilitators

	Characteristics	Strengths	Limitations
The Driver	Pushy, impatient, keeps quite a tight control over the group's direction. The Driver tends to decide when to move on and the group tends to respond to the questions and suggestions made.	Brings energy to the group The end task is usually delivered Group kept on their toes and on track	The group do not take responsibility and therefore become dependent of the facilitator The group are at the whim of the facilitator and less able to face new challenges themselves This is less like facilitation but more like managing and controlling the group Style can be threatening and therefore the group may feel inhibited in contributing
The Inquisitor	Probing, questioning, and relying solely on this approach for handling groups. They continually ask questions, rather than reveal their own thoughts and when put on the spot by a question, turn it back to the questioner.	Helps groups to think things through for themselves Does not impose his/her ideas on the group Keeps the responsibility for ideas and decisions within the group	Can seem like the Spanish inquisition with question after question Can create a distant, aloof relationship with the group, by not revealing what they are really thinking or feeling, therefore not seem human Purely relying on questions can frustrate groups, particularly if they cannot decipher what the facilitator is trying to draw out.

	Characteristics	Strengths	Limitations
The Empathiser	Sensitive and supportive, the empathiser is concerned with the relationships within the groups and adopts a warm, caring and nurturing style with the group. Their interventions are characterised by asking individuals how they feel and encouraging the group to share their feelings and emotions	Stimulates groups to recognise feelings and emotions as well as encouraging them to reveal their true thoughts and feelings. Gets close to the group and therefore really begins to understand them as individuals. Ensures conflicts and disagreements are not overlooked or unaddressed	The approach can be irritating and therefore discourage the group from exploring process issues to any extent. They can become obsessed with relentlessly exploring issues which they feel are important rather than ensuring responsibility for issues remains with the group. Their preoccupation with emotions can distract them from the task at hand.
The Expert	Tends to be influential with the group, constantly bringing their experiences and advice to the group. The expert has been there and done it all before, they rely on anecdotes and models as their interventions.	Providing that the inputs are relevant, groups can benefit from the external stimulus the expert brings. Creates a level of reassurance and confidence with the group as they feel they are in safe hands.	Groups tend to become dependent on the expert, consequently seeking their ideas and answers. The expert's previous experience and solutions are not necessarily appropriate to this situation. The effectiveness of their interventions can be easily dismissed due to the impact of their 'know it all' style.

The Expert (continued)		The anecdotes can strike a cord with the group as they begin to recognise the relevance of the anecdote to themselves and modify their behaviour as necessary.	
The Pleaser	Keen to build relationships with all groups and most concerned with harmony and not 'rocking the boat', the Pleaser is preoccupied with being liked and popular and will say whatever they need to, to keep everyone happy.	Easily accepted by the group, due to their warm and non-threatening style. Groups enjoy their company, particularly as they will often bring humour to group settings. Their interventions are readily accepted by the group because they express them in unobstructive and palatable ways.	Their desire for harmony means they tend not to confront issues. The first sign of any conflict or disagreement is smoothed over with humour which serves to distract from the issue, rather than resolve it. Their desire to please can cause them to bottle up their own feelings and emotions and therefore cause the internal build up of frustration and tension.
The Super Group Member	Their eagerness to help means that they readily cross over from facilitator to group member. They join the group, contribute ideas and share the responsibility for taking actions.	Can help struggling groups with ideas and suggestions. Can often bring energy and enthusiasm to groups.	Groups can often become confused as to their role. Their involvement in the group tends to reduce the degree to which they can stand back and encourage the group to examine their effectiveness.

The Super-Group Member (continued)		Adopting this role can enable inexperienced facilitators to gather confidence with the group.	They can create the role of expert for themselves which causes the group to become over-reliant on them.

Facilitator Baggage

The skills of facilitation at one level are logical, even if somewhat challenging; however, the art of applying these skills demands much practise and review. Interestingly, it is not just the group with whom the facilitator might be battling with as they seek to refine and develop these skills; they themselves often provide the largest barriers to successful skill application.

Every facilitator is constantly receiving messages from inside their own head: *"there's a problem here, you need to intervene; go for it"*, all of which serve to condition the facilitator's behaviour. Unfortunately, these messages do not solely stimulate action. Some messages act as barriers, restraints or pressures upon us. This pressure is often termed 'baggage' as it places constraints upon us in such a way as to significantly or unhelpfully raise our anxiety, inhibit our contribution and stifle good facilitation.

A typical example is *"I have to gain credibility and demonstrate my skill by getting it right first time."* In reality, it is nearly impossible to get every intervention right first time. The real skill is the facilitator's ability to review and recover the intervention, rather than beat themselves senseless with messages of failure which only serve to undermine the facilitator's competence. This then has the impact of raising their anxiety levels even further as they place even more pressure on themselves to not only get it right first time, but also to do it in such a way that its effect more than compensates for the initial failure as well as building their confidence and credibility again with the group.

Facilitators carry a vast array of baggage; some of the typical examples are captured below:

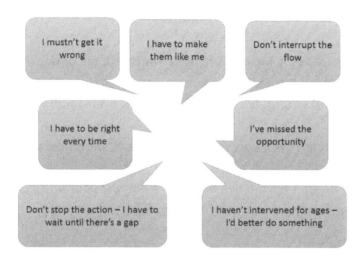

Underlying this baggage are a number of insecurities: the fear of failure, the fear of looking stupid and the fear of uncertainty and ambiguity, each of which serve to undermine the facilitator's confidence and thus their effectiveness.

How can this baggage be overcome?

The fact that there is baggage, means there are no simple answers, however, recognising that it is baggage is the first step towards limiting its impact. By bringing these issues from the sub-conscious to the conscious, may not immediately enthuse one to take on the challenge but it does bring the dilemma into the limelight and provide individuals with clear areas for development.

For some facilitators they have sought to counter the negative lead messages with positive thoughts, thereby seeking to minimise the degree to which these undermine their confidence.

Typical counter messages are:

"Go for it, what's the worst that can go wrong? Does it really matter?"

"It's only facilitation, not a matter of life or death"

"If you get it wrong, tell them – they might even value your honesty"

"Be honest with your feelings, they can't deny how you feel"

"If the group respond negatively, it's not just your mistake, there's learning in the way in which they have responded, for them"

3

The Review Process

Much has been written by management theorists and applied by management practitioners in the fields of planning, organising, delegating, motivating, etc, but little attention has been given to the skills of reviewing. It can be argued that this is singularly the most important skill for managers, in that this allows the past to be examined, the present to be established and for the future to be prepared. Reviewing supports planning, organising, delegating etc, by establishing what has been achieved and therefore what direction needs to be taken.

In many ways, this skill underpins all other management competencies; without effective review processes no manager can establish the effectiveness of their planning, or the quality of their skills of delegation.

Why is the Review Process Neglected?

For many practitioners, reviewing is synonymous with dealing with the unknown. It is a process of attending to feelings, concerns, views and opinions and therefore can seem uncomfortable and intangible. For others, it is a loose and unstructured process of grappling with air rather than a results' focused task to be achieved.

In the challenging and tough environments of the commercial world, many managers regard review as a distraction from achieving the task, rather than regarding review as a means for ensuring the task is achieved. It is unwisely seen as time-consuming, energy sapping and drawing attention away from the job in hand. Successful review processes undoubtedly enable teams to achieve rather than stifle the immensely pressured and task focused nature of the working environment. Stopping to think and reflect is often naively regarded as a luxury and referred to derisively with terms such as 'navel contemplation'. Yet in other worlds, review is a fundamental success.

In the world of sport, football teams spend enormous amounts of time prior and post activity, establishing what should happen, what did happen, the degrees of success, and the causes of failure. In professional basketball, during play, coaches use time-outs at key points to gather the team together to review and agree strategies for going forward. In neither of these situations, is review synonymous with time wasting. In each instance, it enables the plans to be assessed, reassessed and revised, individual roles to be re-assigned and goals to be reset or reaffirmed.

In these environments, working is not just about doing, more importantly it is about thinking and reflecting before doing. Unfortunately, all too often in the businessworld, doing is misguidedly regarded as achieving, despite the fact that no great idea or creation comes from doing; they tend to stem from thinking and reflecting.

What is the Review Process?

Quite simply, the review process is the time taken out from the intensity of an activity to establish exactly what has been achieved in both positive and negative terms and what could be the next appropriate steps. This may be a project team examining their current effectiveness and progress against their plan, a management team seeking to establish the strengths and limitations of their working practices, or an individual measuring their effectiveness and performance.

Stereotypically, the review process is most associated with retrospection, looking back on what is happening, what caused things to happen and where one might be now. More importantly, the review process provides the platform for looking forward, by examining the past, establishing the current practice and planning the way ahead.

Kolb's learning cycle graphically demonstrates the importance of review.

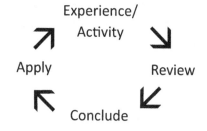

In examining the learning cycle, Kolb stressed the importance attributed to each stage; undertaking activity after activity provides plenty of opportunities and data for learning, but without a halt in the proceedings and the chance to review, little of the activity will be reflected upon. Few conclusions, if any, will be reached, no changes in working practices or behaviour are likely to be initiated and therefore little or nothing will be gleaned from the experience.

Furthermore, time spent reviewing will achieve little if conclusions are not reached and finally, there is little point in reviewing and concluding if the salient points are not applied in the next experience.

When Do You Review?

1. Post activity reviews

The concept of review is most readily associated as the activity that ensues after something has been completed. In this scenario, post activity reviewing enables all experiences to be captured, individual and teams to fully reflect upon their actions and reach conclusions for future tasks. However, post activity reviewing can do little to assist the task in hand; it allows the wonders of hindsight to come to the fore. It can be something of an anticlimax as having immersed all their energies in the activity, most teams are then reluctant to examine what has taken place either through fatigue or fear that it may reveal problems which they can now do little about, in effect, post-activity reviewing is often too late.

2. Pre-activity reviews

Reviewing prior to undertaking activities can provide an invaluable platform in preparing for task achievement, however, few teams give sufficient attention to this stage. All too often, faced by a task dangling in front of them, their enthusiasm, determination and impatience tend to overcome their desire to plan and the team launches itself headlong into activity, often without sufficient thought. Pre-activity reviewing, in effect is part of the planning process, it enables teams to reflect on their past experiences and establish the safeguards which will guide their behaviour and performance to their desired goals.

Reviewing at this stage also enables the objectives to be established and any assumptions or misunderstandings to be clarified as well as a plan for task accomplishment to be agreed. Although this is a planning process, pre-activity reviewing enables wider data to be considered in planning the way ahead. Rarely do teams consider the problems, difficulties and successes in the past as a means of guiding them in the future.

3. Planned reviews

Planning reviews into the task enables groups to take time out and reflect upon the quality of their practices, their interactions and progress towards their goal. It is invaluable as the conclusions of these discussions can influence the direction of the group during the task and subsequently the task outcomes. This is a formal process agreed in advance by the group and usually determined by either set times or set milestones of task accomplishment. Although, as stressed, it can serve to keep the group on track, it can at times be seen as a distraction from the job in hand. All too often, groups immersed in the task resent having to stop and reflect upon their progress to date. Equally those who do stop with good intentions, all too often treat the review process superficially, by quickly checking they are on track and hastily resorting back into the task rather than capitalising on the learning opportunities. The review identifies the strengths of the ways in which they are working and addresses any unhelpful behaviours or working practices.

4. Spontaneous reviews

These reviews, often referred to as "here and now reviews", are unplanned and stimulated by impending success or failure. Fundamentally, spontaneous reviews require groups to stop the action and examine current behaviour and practices. They are similar to planned reviews in that if conducted effectively they can still influence the group's behaviour during task accomplishment; however, they differ in that they are not planned for in advance. In effect, they occur on the spur of the moment and can be introduced by any group member. They are usually stimulated by problems being experienced within the group that are not being addressed to such an extent that individuals recognise the need to stop and rethink the ways in which they are working.

As already stressed, they are most readily initiated at moments of crisis; however, they can be equally valid for high performing groups in recognising how their behaviour or working practices are contributing to success. This enables the group to consciously adhere to certain working practices or behaviours and potentially achieve even more.

How Do You Review?

Reviews can be undertaken in one of three key ways:

1. Structured reviews

In this scenario, groups review their behaviours and working practices against a number of specific questions, e.g:

- *What was the leadership like in the group?*
- *Who was the most influential team member?*
- *What was the level of participation?*

The review is structured in that the questions provide a clear focus for the issues to be addressed. They are relatively unambiguous and provide very specific responses. This type of review is most appropriate for immature groups, i.e. groups that have spent little time together, or are not as yet used to reviewing. They are unable, at the moment, to be rigorous and objective in examining the group behaviour and require the specific questions to stimulate their thinking.

Structured reviews tend to encourage control of the review process to remain with the facilitator. The real challenge for the facilitator is to raise the group's ability to undertake honest reviews at the same time as reducing dependency upon them as the facilitator.

2. Semi-structured reviews

These are similar to structured reviews in that groups review themselves against a series of questions. However, semi- structured review questions are much broader and less specific than those posed during structured reviews, e.g:

- *In what ways did the group work well?*
- *How could the group enhance the way in which it worked?*

This type of review works most appropriately with groups who have experienced reviewing, but as yet are unable to fully take on the reviews for themselves, or to create their own structure. The semi-structured review provides a framework to stimulate thinking and allow groups to reach their own conclusions, rather than targeting the group towards specific learning points which tends to be the effect of the structured review process.

3. Unstructured reviews

In this instance, the group is provided with no framework whatsoever. The group engages in the review process and creates the agenda and framework for themselves.

The ownership and control of the review process rests squarely with the group and thus this type of review is most appropriately applied to groups which have reached a high level of maturity. By this, we mean they are able to examine their own behaviour and working practices in a very objective and robust way and do so spontaneously without the prompting of facilitators.

Structuring the Review Process

As described previously in the Kolb model, the review process is fundamental to the learning process. Yet all too often, the review process is applied in a loose and ambiguous way and this is largely because groups engage in review discussions without any form of framework or direction. Structured and semi-structured reviews can provide the stimulus, however the key to successful reviewing is the art of progressing the responses into conclusions and action.

To assist facilitators and groups to informally structure the review process, two basic structures are described below:

1.

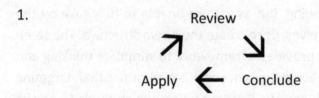

Once the groups have reviewed, they are then invited to agree upon the key conclusions reached and finally the actions they wish to take in relation to these conclusions. During the review, i.e. issue generation stage, a range of issues, views and opinions are discussed. These are subsequently honed down during the conclusions stage and transmitted into a small number of tangible changes in the application stage.

2.

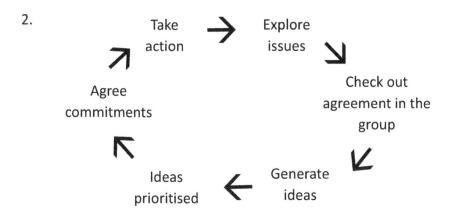

In this framework, once the issues have been explored, agreement is sought in the group as to the accuracy of the diagnosis before ideas are generated and then prioritised. Once the ideas have been prioritised, they are finally tested within the group before these are then translated into commitments and subsequent action.

Methods of Review

"Picturesque"

The Activity

Each team member is invited to take a sheet of flipchart paper and armed with a marker pen, draw one of the following diagrams.

- What they saw as the learning within the task.
- How they felt at different stages during the task.
- How they saw the team develop.

Once completed, each flipchart is posted around the room and each participant has the opportunity to study the diagrams before they are talked through in turn.

Guidelines for Facilitators

This activity requires participants to be spontaneous and uninhibited in their creativity; however, it can be an unthreatening way of encouraging individuals to reveal their thoughts and feelings.

Before selecting this method, one needs to take account of team size, as teams greater than six can result in too much time being consumed in exploring the diagrams, rather than having adequate time and interest to explore the meanings.

To gain full value from the activity, the similarities and differences between differing drawings need to be identified and conclusions reached.

"Shuffle"

The Activity

Each team member is randomly given 12 cards, upon which is written a statement of team behaviour. For example, it might say:

Clear at setting and following its objectives	or	Problem solving and difficulties not aired but avoided

The pack of cards should contain a mixture of positive and negative statements; the distribution of the cards should be random in that some individuals will receive more positive than negative statements and vice versa.

The individual is then asked to consider the team and decide which statement most accurately reflects the way the team has worked.

One at a time, a card is posted on the wall and an explanation given as to why it has been chosen. The role of the team is to explore and discuss the similarities and differences between individuals' perceptions.

Guidelines for Facilitators

This activity is helpful in stimulating individuals to consider the wide variety of behaviours present during a task. Asking individuals to gather their thoughts about the behaviours seen can be challenging particularly for teams which have little experience of both recognising and expressing individual and group behaviour.

In facilitating this activity, one needs to be mindful of the distribution of feedback, ensuring each group member posts a balance of both positive and negative feedback. It is also important to monitor the way in which the conversation is being handled, in that the behaviour being described on the cards is not being replicated during this discussion.

"Animal Magic"

The Activity

Each participant considers each other member of the group and decides from the behaviour they have seen, which animal they most associate with that individual. Then, by working around the room, each individual reveals the animal they have chosen for each of their colleagues, together with their rationale for that selection.

At the end of the activity, each individual summarises the feedback given to them as well as providing their own description of themselves.

Guidelines for Facilitators

This activity can be fun, stimulating and illuminating and particularly useful for groups who may be inhibited in providing direct feedback. In this instance, the group has been asked to consider each other as animals, other variations can be used e.g., cars, holiday destinations, sports, hobbies, etc.

The facilitator may well need to encourage the group members to explain their reasoning; often individuals can readily stereotype each other as animals, but need time and stimulation to recognise the rationale for their conclusions. It is important to balance the humour that this activity can create with the reality of the feedback, and ensure that the key messages are not lost.

"Graphic"

The Activity

Two axes are drawn on a flipchart. The vertical axis is marked high and low; the horizontal axis is segmented by significant stages during the task, e.g. the briefing, the objective setting phase, the planning, the agreement of roles etc.

Each individual plots on the graph the points at which they felt high and low during the activity. Once each individual has drawn their graph, they are invited to explain their rationale for the graph. During the conversation the role of the rest of the group is to question and understand each other's rationale before seeking to identify the similarities and differences between each graph, reaching conclusions and a plan for moving the whole team forward.

Guidelines for Facilitators

The danger with this activity is that it becomes a non-interactive process, with the group sitting back whilst one individual takes the stage, rather than seeing this as an opportunity to identify when the team was working well and when improvements could be made through analysing individuals' highs and lows.

As facilitator, it is important to support the group in identifying the trends across the group and therefore, conclusions on the group dynamics.

"Reveal"

The Activity

Each participant in the group is handed a sheet of paper, upon which a different question is asked on each sheet of paper, e.g:

- In what ways did the team work well?
- What improvements could be made to the teamworking practices?
- At what point was the team really motoring and why?
- What has been the major learning for you from the activity?
- What progress has this team made during the day?

The individual is asked to write their answer on the bottom of the sheet of paper and fold over their response such that it cannot be seen by any other team member and they pass the sheet of paper to their left.

This process continues until such time that each participant has answered all the key questions.

Once this phase is finished, the first question is read out and one member of the group reads through the responses. These are then clarified and discussed with the rest of the group, before agreement is reached and the next question is explored. At the end of the activity, the responses are posted on flipchart to adorn the walls and act as a constant reference point.

Guidelines for Facilitators

It is important to ensure that the number of questions reflect the number of group members and that during the writing phase, individuals do not engage in discussion with each other. Conversations are discouraged as they could influence colleagues' answers in addition to causing unnecessary distraction from what needs to be a considered and thoughtful phase of the activity.

The strength of this activity lies in the quality of individual thinking time, in that individuals produce their own, uninfluenced views, however, there is sometimes complacency in the way in which the subsequent conversations are handled. Individuals can often believe that they have undertaken the hard work writing their statements, and sit back passively to listen to each individual's rendition. In reality, it is the subsequent conversations that draws real meaning and as a result, learning.

"Measurement"

The Activity

Prior to undertaking a task, the group are asked to consider and agree a set of criteria against which they can measure the effectiveness of their teamwork.

Having agreed the criteria, this is posted on the wall of the syndicate room for all to see. The group subsequently undertakes the task in hand and at an appointed moment, halts their proceedings in order that each person has some individual time to reflect upon the way in which the group has worked. They are then invited to rate the group on a scale of 1-10, where 1 represents less effective and 10 represents very effective, against each of the criteria previously set.

Once the individual has completed this phase, each person writes up their score against each criterion before the group explores the rationale for each previous decision. The group then agrees upon the criteria requiring most attention during the next activity, in addition to recognising which criteria they are currently most competent in achieving.

Guidelines for Facilitators

It is important that the facilitator encourages the group to produce the initial criteria in behavioural terms, as this may lead to confusion and much subjectivity during the measurement phase. For example, rather than saying *we must communicate well*, this needs to be broken down into the component parts, e.g. *when ideas are expressed, we must listen and clarify understanding rather than immediately point out the flaws in the ideas and we must summarise what has been said.*

It is also important to discourage groups from becoming embroiled in negotiating whether a particular criterion should be rated 7 or 8, but encourage the group to seek the trends and principles in making their assessments.

"Which Programme"

The Activity

Which programme provides opportunities for groups to articulate their experiences in a fun and imaginative way? Groups that have experienced tough sessions and thoroughly explored the why's and wherefore's, can increase their energy levels by using this activity.

Each individual is asked to describe the group in terms of a TV character, programme or film. Then, in turn, the individual describes their programme and the reasons for choosing it. Once each individual has completed this, the group summarises the common themes, before each group member indicates which programme or film they would like the group to be in future.

Guidelines for Facilitators

This can be fun and spontaneous, however, with some groups, this will need encouragement. Once started, groups tend to stimulate each other and can become so embroiled in the humour of the activity that the reasons for each choice and the subsequent learning can be lost without the attentiveness of the facilitator.

Challenges in Facilitating Reviews

These examples have been acquired from working with many facilitators over numerous years, and are all, without exception, real examples.

Think about the key challenges or issues for you as a facilitator in each example and what you might do to help the team move forwards.

1. During the review, the facilitator asks questions; the group answers, the facilitator asks the next question, the group answers, no more, no less.

   What are the issues?
   What do you do?

2. This is the first opportunity for the group to review its effectiveness. You choose a semi-structured review and provide the group with some broad questions. The individuals scan the questions and begin to answer them in a bland and superficial way, e.g. when asked how did you work together they answer "fine", "ok", "no problem".

   What are the issues?
   What do you do?

3. During the review, the group debates and raises issues, however, during the ensuing activity, nothing changes. The issues keep exhibiting themselves.

   What are the issues?
   What do you do?

4. The group have been undertaking a task and reach the review phase at which point, they turn and look at you as the facilitator.

   What are the issues?
   What do you do?

5. Individuals acknowledge the need to give feedback to each other, so starting with one individual, the others begin to give feedback to each other and the feedback moves backwards and forwards across the group.

What are the issues?
What do you do?

6. An individual suggests that they hold the review in the bar where they can relax and it can be informal. Others agree.

   What are the issues?
   What do you do?

7. The facilitator is standing at the flipchart and says to the group "I'd like you to think of your current feelings, starting with these" and then proceeds to write up what Anne says. "Now, Andy?" and at the end says "Now let me give you my observations".

   What are the issues?
   What do you do?

8. Individuals say they cannot think of anything.

   What are the issues?
   What do you do?

9. It is just after lunch (or the start of the day, or just before lunch, or at the end of the day). The group are putting little effort into the review and say "well it is the graveyard session".

   What are the issues?
   What do you do?

Suggested Approaches

1. The issues:

   In this instance, the group would appear to be dependent upon the facilitator, in that they are relying on him/her as the form of stimulus doing the Review. Furthermore, they seem to be taking little if any responsibility for the review, in effect they are compliant, responding to what is being asked but doing little to take the questions on and debate with each other. It creates the impression that they are operating at a level whereby they give just enough to get by.

   ### Suggested Approaches

   a. Raise the issues directly with them, by explaining what you see happening and asking them why, encourage them to commit to behaving differently.

   b. Adopt a semi-structured review by providing them with a series of questions and then ask them to consider these individually before returning to the group to debate the issues. This will encourage individuals to develop their own views from which they can debate. Then leave them so that they recognise that this discussion is their responsibility, not yours.

   c. Be absent from the early stages of the next review. You may worry that it will fall flat; however, if they have been through a number of reviews already, then potentially they have the experience to succeed. Furthermore, this is more likely to encourage the group to reach a higher level of maturity in the way in which they are working.

2. The issues:

As this is the group's first review, there is likely to be some resistance in saying exactly what they think as they begin to build trust with each other. However, despite this nervousness, their answers demonstrate little or no thought and if this is not attended to, then it could set the tone for future reviews.

Suggested Approaches

a. Explain to the group the importance and value of the review process, share your observations about their responses and encourage them to give more thought to the way in which they have worked.

b. Probe their responses and ask more specific questions.

c. Explain the importance of the review process and suggest they spend a few moments gathering their thoughts together.

d. If the activity has been videoed, suggest they watch the video and make notes of how they see the group working as a means of stimulating their thinking.

3. The issues:

It would appear that the group has a level of objectivity and rigour to identify the issues, so the challenge here is less about honesty, but more about application. Despite all good intentions, they fail to be able to modify their behaviour or actions next time around.

Firstly, establish why it is that their good intentions fail to result in a change of action. Is it that they truly don't understand how to behave differently, do they get so emerged in that they lose sight or some of the processes needs or are they not really committed to operating differently?

Suggested Approaches

a. *Lack of understanding*. Review their understanding of what is required and ensure each person describes how they could operate differently.

b. *Too task focused*. Have their behavioural commitments written up and placed on the wall and then encourage them to adopt planned reviews at regular intervals during the task. This could enable them to stop and think during the task and thereby encourage them to focus upon their process issues.

c. *Lack of commitment*. Establish exactly why they are less committed. Is it that they are quite happy operating as they are, or is it that they see no point in examining the process? If so, one could either challenge these responses directly, or engage in a debate with the group encouraging them to question their commitment.

4. The issues:

   The group have completed the task and one might presume they have taken some degree of ownership for this. However, by turning to look at you as the facilitator, the implication is that it is now time to review and therefore they seem to imply this is your responsibility.

   Suggested Approaches

   a. If the group have conducted a number of effective reviews previously, turn the issue back to them, by either asking them how they intend to review or by indicating that it is the review phase and temporarily leave the room. In both instances, ownership and responsibility is passed back to the group.

b. If you believe the group needs some support, provide them with a semi-structured review by posing a number of key questions. Leave them to start the review process on their own, before returning to provide any further support.

c. Alternatively ask them to choose from the variety of review methods described previously.

5. The issues:

If the feedback is of good quality, the disparate process that the group seem to be working to is likely to dilute the impact of the feedback. By moving randomly to and fro between individuals, it is likely that the key themes for each individual may be lost. Furthermore, it is likely that there will be either an imbalance of feedback to different individuals, or unequal positive or negative feedback and this will be difficult to track without a structured process.

Suggested Approaches

a. Stress your concerns and suggest they focus on one individual at a time.

b. Allow the group to continue working in their spontaneous and unstructured manner, however, at regular intervals, encourage each individual to summarise what they have learned from the feedback to date.

c. At an appropriate moment, ask the group to review how well they are working together and to summarise the feedback that has been given to others as a way of testing the effectiveness of their current working methods.

6. The issues:

If the group conducts their review in the bar, assuming that others have access to this area, then it is likely that there will be a number of distractions and interferences. Furthermore although this could encourage the discussions to be relaxed and informal it is unlikely to encourage any sensitive issues to be raised or problems confronted, and the quality and value of the review will be significantly undermined.

This leads on to wonder why there is such reluctance to review there and then in their current environment. It could be that they do want more informality however this could be the means for avoiding the real issues at stake.

Suggested Approaches

a. Ask the group to think through the impact and consequences of using a communal area for discussing what could be sensitive issues.

b. Stress your concern with reviewing in the bar and ask the group how they could create a relaxed and informal environment where they are currently working.

c. Ask the group what worked well and what got in the way during previous reviews. By so doing one is able to establish whether their reluctance to review here and now is a reflection of previous experiences or an innocent request.

7. The issues:

The Facilitator is creating dependency upon him/herself by directing the proceedings. The group may be a new or immature group and may be in need of some guidance; however, this seems more to do with control than guidance. Furthermore, by writing upon the flipchart themselves, they are in danger of forcing themselves to interpret what is being said as well as regimenting each person's contribution by indicating when they would like each group member to contribute. Finally by introducing their own perceptions as facilitator at the end of each discussion could elevate themselves to expert, by providing the 'correct perceptions' as a means of summary.

Suggested Approaches

a. The facilitator passes the responsibility for writing on the flipchart to the group and leaves them to continue without the facilitator's involvement.

b. The facilitator passes the responsibility for writing on the flipchart to the group and then contributes occasionally.

c. The facilitator agrees the framework for reviewing with the group.

8. The issues:

Individuals and groups often claim that they cannot think of anything and this may be true. Therefore if that is the case, the challenge is to raise the group's awareness of the process at play and draw into their consciousness the dynamics in order that they have sufficient data to conduct effective reviews. However, all too often, individuals and groups use their supposed inability to recall, to hide their fears and concerns about being open and honest. It is also to easy to claim that they cannot think of anything in particular when these are underlying issues which might cause discomfort if confronted.

Suggested Approaches

a. Stress the importance of feedback and suggest they spend some individual time considering a number of key questions.

b. Be prepared to provide the group with your own observations and encourage the group members to discuss and debate these.

c. Challenge the group's reluctance to review and discuss its effectiveness. In reality, no group can think of nothing. There will always be aspects worth considering, whether they are positive or negative.

9. The issues:

   Groups are all too ready to attribute their lack of enthusiasm, energy or commitment during the review process, as being fuelled by the time of the day. In reality, although groups may be weary, it is all too often a reflection of the unstimulating processes that they are adopting, particularly as group members all too often seem to be able to summon energy later in the day for extra curricular activities.

Suggested Approaches

a. Confront the group's dynamics and processes and encourage them to identify more stimulating ways of working.

b. Allow the groups space to gather their energies before encouraging them to identify more stimulating ways of working.

c. Acknowledge that it is the graveyard session and ask the group how they can overcome this bearing in mind what needs to be achieved.

4

Line Manager As Facilitator

For years facilitation has been regarded as the black art for trainers; closely guarded, shrouded in mystery; a club for exclusive members only. Hardly surprisingly, line managers have given the skill a wide berth and, in fairness to them, they have been encouraged to do so by those who have developed the skill. Not that I believe that all and sundry can facilitate well, nor do I believe that standards of facilitation should be lowered so that it is easy to do, however I do believe that we as practitioners should enable others to learn and develop the skills – they are not sacred. That said, all line managers need to behave in ways in which they engage their teams to take responsibility for issues, problems and solutions.

The fundamental skills that underpin good facilitation: listening, questioning, observing, expressing your feelings, clarifying and suggesting are clearly not exclusive to this intervention. Line managers are applying these skills throughout the business world, perhaps not in the same combinations or in the same contexts that have been described, nor with the audacious title of facilitator! For the many however, they fail to recognise this and the facilitator propaganda, laced with war stories of individuals becoming emotional, tends to reinforce that this is the skill of a few and should not be the skill of many.

Why are line managers becoming business facilitators?

To encourage greater team-working and create new cultures and environments with flatter structures.	The pressure upon line managers is intensifying. In the past a manager had his team and was able to manage them on a day to day basis. Now, flatter structures have resulted in many managers having to manage a number of teams. Clearly, this is no new concept but what is clear is that the ability to manage in its truest sense is impossible. Managers are having to encourage teams to take on responsibility for the decision making and management of their respective business units.

Their role is not to set the pace, lead and galvanise the team into action but to facilitate the teams through the process of self-direction. One may wonder whether we are creating some form of hippy commune; far from it. We are moving towards autonomous work teams, whose rigour of thinking, decision making, ownership and sense of responsibility drives them to achieve new heights.

One can be forgiven for thinking that the concept of managing a number of teams is not new; in the retail sector there have been regional or area managers since time began. However the focus and style of the role has been fundamentally different. In the past, the job incumbents have operated more as policemen, upholding the company's policies and practices, demanding |

	adherence and encouraging their managers to live out this role model. Their focus has been primarily on their direct reports i.e. the indivdual and not the team. Bill was recently appointed General Manager for a number of car dealerships; previously he was General Manager of one dealership, now he was responsible for five. His former role was not filled nor were the vacancies created by his four colleagues moving on. Instead the remaining team absorbed the responsibilities and accountabilities and Bill's role was to support these teams to drive the five dealerships forward, not to drive them himself as he had in the past. Clearly this required a significant shift in his behaviour and approach: no longer could he take control, make the decisions, create the drive and energy; instead he had to help the teams to take responsibility for their dealerships and facilitate them through the challenges ahead.
To encourage greater ownership and transfer of learning into the workplace.	A number of HRD functions in leading UK companies have recognised the power and influence of line managers becoming more actively involved in the delivery of training and development initiatives. In fact in one organisation, line managers facilitate 90% of development programmes either working with line manager colleagues or training and development practitioners.

	For years we have been fed the importance of line managers owning their own development and engendering their commitment to the development of their own team. For years they have been excluded from the learning their team members experience on residential programmes. Their role has been often limited to pre and post course briefing and the very thought of them facilitating events has been dismissed either for our or their fear in delivering, or the overly exploited excuse of time.
To grow and develop their own teams	The concept of facilitating the growth of your own team has been readily dismissed by practitioners. All too often the idea of the manager as facilitator has conjured up a picture of managers juggling between the two roles and failing miserably. Besides, it questions the simplistic notion of the facilitator as some independent, dispassionate being. Unfortunately, if we truly believe in the concept of empowerment and believe that teams can drive their own learning, then equipping the manager with the skills to support this is fundamental. This is not to suggest that this is not a particularly demanding role. This is far from the truth, it requires managers to develop exceptional levels of self and other's awareness and requires high levels of sensitivity to group processes and above all a willingness to talk

	about their own feelings. However despite these demands, experiences of this work in the last few years have demonstrated unreservedly the power of facilitating your own team's development.
To encourage more effective working with project teams and peer group	The need for cross-functional teams, project team-working, focus groups etc is continually growing within organisations as is the need to find more effective solutions to problems as well as greater invention and commitment to the decision-making process. In these environments the need for individuals to take on the role of facilitator from within the team is increasing. This is not to say that everyone should be facilitating at once, nor is any one person deemed to be the facilitator, or the role rotated round the group; instead it is the ability of each of the individuals to draw upon their facilitator skills to address problems and issues that emerge within the team's dynamics. One could argue that this is merely good team-working skills and strictly speaking this is true. but only with the onset of facilitation have individuals been equipped with the skills to manage these conversations successfully.

The myths of managers as facilitators

They won't be interested	Many but not all managers are keen or excited by the challenges that facilitation offers. For some it is a welcome alternative from the day to day challenges in the workplace; for others it provides real opportunities to stretch and develop themselves. Common to the most successful facilitators is a fundamental interest and commitment to the development of others.
They won't have the skills	Many of the skills used by facilitators are regularly used by managers in the workplace although they may not be readily seen as such. Nevertheless many managers are surprised at the similarities between the behaviour required on a programme and those applied in the workplace, particularly questioning, listening, challenging and expressing their feelings. This is not to say that all managers can facilitate, nor that all managers have the natural ability to do so, in reality prior to any development event, our experiences have shown that providing managers with the opportunities to practise and develop their skills in a safe environment through a facilitation programme significantly enhances not only their skills but their self-confidence and as a result their willingness to push themselves into challenging situations.
They will dominate and be insensitive	Clearly this is a possibility not just for line managers but trainers alike and largely is reflection of their personality and disposition. In reality our experiences seem to indicate much to the contrary. Most line managers are so pre-occupied with not dominating that they significantly inhibit their

	effectiveness by holding back too much and letting issues pass too readily. It seems that many managers carry mental messages which start with the words don't do… don't do… rather than do… do… and hardly surprisingly many can become paralysed for fear of causing difficulties.
They will use any information gleaned to their own advantage	Trust and confidentiality are fundamental to any development initiative. The ability of facilitators to build relationships with groups and individuals significantly influences the effectiveness of the interactions. Without doubt the involvement of line managers in development initiatives can stimulate initial inhibitions and reservations within groups and with individuals, however few of them recognise the risks and personal challenges that line managers take in facilitation. Information gained by the group about the line manager can be equally abused and it is for this reason that confidentiality pacts between the various parties tend to address these issues. This is not to create the impression that all facilitators are sweetness and light, however any doubts or uncertainties and trust and confidentiality must be readily confronted.

The challenges in developing line managers as facilitators

Giving them belief	Despite the confidence line managers often portray in their day to day roles in the workplace, most seem to approach facilitation with both excitement and trepidation as their anxieties and uncertainties take hold. Their desire to do a good job is matched by their fear of losing credibility. Unfortunately this anxiety is often increased by trainers who create myths and mystique around the world of facilitation. Fundamentally line managers need support and encouragement (as well as honest and sensitive feedback), to overcome any doubts or uncertainties they may carry with them as baggage.
Example	*Christine used a couple of interventions which didn't go as well as she had hoped: the large group rejected them. Because they didn't work well she lost confidence and withdrew, made excuses to be out of the group, making phone calls. We had to handle her carefully; we discussed with her what she'd done and explored her reasons. We then prompted her to make interventions in the smaller groups and have small wins before going back into the larger group.*
Overcoming war stories	New managers/facilitators seem to embark upon the development process with the most extreme facilitation problems lodged in their minds. They may have never personally experienced a tough facilitation situation particularly themselves, nor met anyone who has, however they seem to believe that intense conflict, highly charged emotional situations,

	and individuals having traumatic experiences are the norm. The managers seem to become pre-occupied with either worries of what should they do in this situation or what support available to the individuals themselves. In reality few of the stories are strictly true, many have been enhanced to increase the fascination and interest levels. Furthermore, rarely will they face the problems themselves, more importantly the facilitation team should be selected to have the combined experience to handle both extremes.
Example	*Simon was very nervous and pessimistic about his ability. In any type of group situation he envisaged, he always assumed the worst possible thing that could happen. Trying to deal with him at a logical level was of little effect: he said 'ah well, it could be this or that...' He only made changes in his behaviour when he started getting feedback that he was pessimistic all the time.*
Releasing Control	For years line managers have been groomed to take control, provide direction and inspiration; rarely have they been guided to lead from behind, to adopt a low profile and to encourage others to take the lead and to gain satisfaction from watching others succeed. For many line managers, facilitation requires a shift in their day to day behaviours although many have the potential to facilitate well without concentrating on their own behaviour. They have a tendency to lapse into taking control. Rarely does it manifest itself in a domineering or

	arrogant way. Usually it is far more subtle, providing support or encouragement for others and opinions they agree with or providing certainty at times of uncertainty.
Example	*Laura was used to controlling things; she was experienced and knowledgeable, physically a big woman, people deferred to her all the time: what she said went. Her size had an impact – it was imposing and when people came up with ideas in front of her, she would look at them and her eyes would say "I can six flaws in that already". If you weren't 100% clear of your plans, she would close things down immediately. She intervened in ways which were very opinionated"* *In order for her to recognise this, we recorded her behaviour in groups and helped her see this for herself as well as providing very direct and descriptive feedback!*

Case Studies

Occupational Health Nurses

With the levels of pressure and challenge in their roles, it was felt that stress workshops could assist individuals in managing their anxiety and stress levels. The fundamental concept of the workshops was to increase self-help medicine and remove the dependency for one's health from the nurses, doctors etc to the individual. It was felt that by moving this responsibility, individuals would be more willing to consider the importance of their health and increase their readiness to deal with the causes rather than the symptoms. This attitudinal shift coincided with the progressive thinking in the world of pharmacy, which through education is attempting to reduce individuals' dependency on pills and potions which mask the symptoms of the problems but never deal with the root cause. The holistic medicine which looks at the whole you and is concerned with not only your attitude but your whole way of life is seen as the most productive way forward.

The nurses worked through a three day facilitation programme which provided them with opportunities to develop their own skills and style of facilitation. The stress workshops proved to be particularly successful but not without much effort and application. Some individuals refused to face up to and recognise that stress existed or even that they could possibly now or in the future be affected by this. Through their new found facilitation skills they were able to support and challenge participants through this process. This was an incredible shift in skill as most had experienced no previous interpersonal development nor had they been particularly used to handling groups, never mind facilitate workshops. Subsequently to the workshops it has emerged that the nurses have started to apply these skills on much wider settings. It appears that traditionally tedious Health & Safety meetings have become more effective through process interventions. This is not to create the impression that they have all become high powered super facilitators. However their new found confidence has enabled them to draw out issues as well as encouraging potential conflict to emerge and be dealt with rather than simmer beneath the surface.

Facilitating with your own team

Chris led a team of specialists in site identification and acquisition as well as a number of administrators and secretaries in the Property Division of a long established multi-national organisation. For some time he had recognised that his team could work more effectively together. He attended a facilitation programme for Team Leaders which provided him with the skills to draw out the team issues and support the team through the development process.

Historically the concept of the line manager facilitating within their own team had been rejected in that it is both too challenging for the manager to retain his/her objectivity, and may inhibit his/her contributions at a content level to the debates and decisions. However our work over many years has enabled line managers to adopt the skills of the facilitator into their everyday roles rather than falling into a formal facilitation role.

Chris returned to his team and discussed with them the notion of an away day which with their agreement he duly designed. Through breaking the team of ten into smaller groups, a wide range of issues emerged, some that he was aware of, a number which were new. Chris describes how his major challenge was to draw out the more junior members of the team who were uncertain of the value of their own contribution to the process. He said that although this was tough, towards the afternoon the team became much looser with each other. Although he did make contributions, he tended to listen more and encouraged the team to talk openly about the way they were both in the work place and here and now. Future follow up days created greater team unity, together with more robust working practices, and Chris talked about how pleased he was with the growth of the team in terms of its honesty, openness and support for each other. Even the most junior members of the team took responsibility for encouraging review discussions and confronting issues. In response Chris' facilitation skills started to be spread amongst the team. The effect of this led to the team handling a particularly gruelling schedule with ease and simplicity. In the past this had been fraught with conflicts and back biting and had resulted in constantly slipping projects and dissatisfied clients.

Line managers facilitating programmes

Neil was sponsor of a development programme for middle managers; in this role he co-facilitated the programme in addition to supporting group members back in the workplace. Initially he approached the facilitation process with caution, concerned not to damage the learning process. Through regular reviews in which Neil received support, encouragement, guidance and challenge, he began to be less inhibited in discussions with the groups, their processes and challenging the attitudes and behaviours of participants. His understanding of their work environment enabled him to challenge ingrained thinking. Through the opportunity to facilitate, Neil talked of his own learning development, both at a skill level and his understanding of the current pressure facing managers further down the hierarchy in his own function. This led him to go back in to his own team and re-examine the pressures and working practices.

As a line manager within the function, Neil was able to build close on-going relationships with the participants in their support groups and as a result assist them in implementing their development plans. This was addressed when helping them to think through how to make the necessary changes stick as well as using his experience of his business and their line managers to determine how the participants approached their issues. He was also able to use his influence and contacts to arrange secondments.

5

Co-Facilitation

Co-facilitation is the simple concept of two or more facilitators working as a cohesive unit to help others achieve things for themselves. It is no more or less complex than that, so why on earth does such a simple concept become so fraught with difficulties, challenges and problems?

The very skills which facilitators freely bring to groups are essentially the source of the problems. Experienced facilitators tend to have their own styles and ways of handling group processes; rarely is this discussed together and rarely are the ground rules for working established. All too often, co-facilitation is the fascinating art of treading on each other's toes and the resultant process of trying to redress the problems and difficulties in the facilitator team rather than support the group's processes.

A common myth underpinning co-facilitation is that two heads are better than one as they provide support and reassurance to each other. In fact this often lulls facilitators into a false sense of security that two highly skilled facilitators will naturally be able to create synergy in the way in which they work with each other. In reality, it requires higher skill levels than individual facilitation requires, for not only does the co-facilitator have to handle group processes, together with their impact and role within the group, but also be able to manage and support their colleagues interventions.

In individual facilitation, the facilitator is absorbed in the nuances of the group. Add another facilitator for good measure and things provide a more complex dimension as one needs to understand not only the group's behaviour, but also the subsequent interventions of your colleague. This can prove to be the most absorbing and perplexing of activities that challenges the patience of the most adept of facilitators.

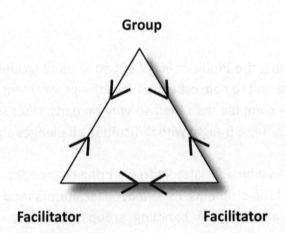

So what does it take to be successful co-facilitators?

Quite simply:

- sensitivity *(an awareness and responsiveness to each other's needs)*

- honesty with each other *(a willingness to state one's own opinion and feelings in ways which attend to others' sensitivity)*

- agreed behavioural groundrules *(agreement as to how you work together)*

In terms of behavioural groundrules, co-facilitators need to agree:

1. how long they will spend with groups;

2. how regularly they will swap groups;

3. how they will communicate with each other;

4. how they will operate if either of them become embroiled in conflict with the group;

5. what to do if both of them are with the group at the same time;

6. who will take responsibility for briefing which scenarios.

For all facilitators, co-facilitation provides tremendous personal growth opportunities and the chance to learn from one another about each other respective styles, impact and effectiveness in working with groups. Without doubt, facilitation is not the art of tricks or techniques, but the skill of being yourself in helping others do things for themselves.

1. How long should the facilitator spend with the groups?

Often, the facilitator's natural inclination is to nestle in the room with the group for the full duration of an activity. This serves to alleviate any anxieties that the facilitator might have, that they may miss something or ensures that they feel they are adding value, even if this is a delusion. More so, it tends to create a level of dependency upon the facilitator, as groups become reliant on the facilitator.

The time spent in the room is clearly fundamental to any group's development coupled with the nature of interventions. Interestingly, the absence of the facilitator can be the trigger for groups to confront issues as they recognise that if they don't deal with problems, no saviour in the form of a facilitator will do so. Thus the fundamental issue of time spent in and out of the group is paramount in facilitator decision-making.

2. How regularly should the facilitators move between groups?

The concept of moving between groups for many facilitators is an anathema. Many believe that the facilitator should remain with one learning group during the duration of a management programme, so building understanding, and supposedly positioning the facilitator to make telling interventions with their wealth of understanding of that group. Unfortunately, remaining with the group for lengthy periods of time can create a level of ownership and protectiveness by the facilitator as they begin to associate the group's success or failure as a reflection of themselves.

Furthermore, moving between groups enables the groups themselves to experience different styles and types of interventions and as a result different forms of stimulation to challenge and develop their effectiveness.

3. How will the facilitators communicate with each other?

Keeping facilitators abreast of the progress each group is making, is crucial in facilitator cohesiveness. Much can be gleaned from colleagues' descriptions of what's been seen and subsequently what they did. More importantly this aids the facilitators' decision-making process by determining what might be the next move for supporting the group's growth.

The communication between facilitators is essential and more often than not is achieved through regular review meetings during the day's activities. Co-facilitation requires individuals committing to meet at appointed times during the day. This serves to provide the facilitation team with the opportunities to share insights and learning as well as generating ideas on how to handle a particular situation. These conversations need to be short and focused allowing the facilitators to re-group before possibly joining new groups.

4. **Who will take responsibility for briefing the activities?**

Clarity of briefing is essential in engendering ownership and commitment to the task. For groups to take responsibility for a task it is important that they recognise not only what is being asked of them: **the purpose;** but also why it's being asked of them: **the importance.**

All too often facilitators provide extensive explanations for what is being asked of the group, and readily assume that this will be sufficient to excite them. A group's motivation to commit to a task is largely determined by their perceived need to do so. The need or importance may have to be sold to the group: it is this which drives the group and sets the failure to achieve its subsequent consequences in context.

5. **How do you operate if either of you as facilitators become embroiled in conflict with the group?**

If your colleague is embroiled in conflict, many facilitators sit back and spectate and all too often rationalise their behaviour by saying: "I didn't want to add to the problems". The last thing your colleague needs is a spectator; more importantly, they need space to reconsider their strategy. Your intervention can be crucial, not in avoiding the issues or brushing them under the carpet, but by possibly reviewing the problem. Fundamentally your role is to support your colleague, not by reinforcing their point of view but by creating space for it to be listened to and heard by the group and then to support your colleague in discussing their response.

6. What do you do if both of you are in the group at the same time?

Allow each other space and time to pursue your respective strategies but most importantly ensure you do not compete with each and that your interventions clearly build upon each other. Competition is one of the fundamental downfalls of co-facilitators; individual egos fighting for space serves only to confuse and alienate groups from the process. Each must be prepared to sit back and allow their colleague to pursue their interventions unless they become embroiled in conflict.

Skills Practice

What do you do if...

1. your colleague makes a statement in the group which you fundamentally disagree with?

2. your colleague becomes embroiled in conflict with the group?

3. a group raises concerns with you about your colleague?

4. your colleague disagrees with what you are saying and expresses this in the group?

5. the group asks you if you are deliberately playing hard and soft facilitator?

6. your colleague's description of what is happening in the group leads you to believe that intervention is required however you seem to be hearing all the justifications for why it is not right to intervene.

7. you are working with the group in one direction and your colleague's intervention takes the group off in another?

8. you are in the group with your colleague and are not sure what to do next?

Possible Solutions

1. If the statement is not going to have a fundamental effect on the programme, allow it to pass and then discuss this with your colleague out of the group later.

   If the statement will significantly impact on the programme, then acknowledge your colleague's view but build in your own. E.g. "As Karen says you could see this like *x*, others may put forward *y*".

   It is important that you do not openly undermine your colleague and equally are not seen to be taking an alternate view as this will only serve to encourage groups to divide you. This could be achieved by describing the alternative view but not letting it be known that it is yours.

2. Review with the group and the facilitator what is happening as a means to ensuring that the group recognise their own behaviour in the conflict and the limitations they are placing on their own

learning. Only later, outside of the group and if necessary, discuss your colleague's interventions. The temptation is to explicitly take sides but in this scenario your behaviour should be perceived as neutral. In reality though your role is to enable your colleague's views to be listened to and heard. Neutrality can often be maintained by intervening through asking questions.

e.g. "I understand that you believe the way in which the point is being delivered is unhelpful, but considering the nature of the point being made, might there be some truth in it?"

"What's happening at the moment? How are you responding to Chris' interventions?

"How are you doing against your ground rules at the moment?"

3. Groups may often confide in you their views about your colleague and their hopes that you will attend to this. However this does little or nothing in helping them to take responsibility for the issues. Faced by this dilemma your role is to help them consider a) what your colleague might have been trying to do and b) how they will handle the issue with him/her and then leave it with them to deal with.

It is then essential that you relay the conversation you have just had to your colleague in order that they can prepare themselves for handling the discussion, together with creating opportunities which allow the group to raise the issues with him/her.

e.g. Allow a short time to pass and then join the group again but wait for them to initiate the conversation with you. If after a number of visits they still do not raise the issues, informally review with the group how the programme is going.

It is important throughout their conversation that there is no indication to suggest that the facilitators have been talking as this will only serve to lessen trust and create suspicion of the facilitator team.

4. Allow this issue to pass, make light of the issue in the group and then rigorously review what's happened outside of the group stating your feelings and the effect on you. Reach agreement on how similar situations can be avoided in the future.

5. Clarify and obtain data on how they have come to those conclusions and state that this is not your intention and that it is interesting that they see it this way. Then review this conversation with your colleague and agree how you will behave mutually during the remainder of the programme.

6. Discuss other ways of handling the same issue, but if on the next occasion your colleague fails to act, raise your concerns about the effect of further inaction in supporting the group's progress.

7. Allow your colleague to explore the new direction and once finished find ways of completing any outstanding issues from your earlier intervention. Then review what happened and agree how this type of situation should be handled in the future.

8. Make eye contact with your colleague and encourage him/her to leave the room with you. This provides you with the opportunity to discuss what you have seen and decide whether it is appropriate or not to do anything, together with agreeing your strategy forgoing forward.

However, if you are faced with the same dilemma in the whole group then it might seem strange for both of you to leave, so suggest a comfort break for the whole group, providing the facilitation team with time and space to discuss the current situation.

Case Study

The group:	Day 2 of a three day management development programme. Working in pairs, the group were supposed to be reviewing each individual's effectiveness as indicated by diagnostic pre-work.
The issues:	The group were dealing with each person's review very superficially: they weren't probing nor adding their own perceptions, instead they were sitting passively listening to each person's monologue and rationalising their pre-work results. e.g. x doesn't know me very well! y's a poor performer, so they would say that any way!
Interventions:	The first facilitator challenged the group's complacency and suggested they were going through the motions of the task in hand without grasping all the learning opportunities available. This had the effect of shocking the group, and their immediate response was to become defensive and reject the facilitator's intervention. Once the facilitator had left the group, although annoyed they began to reflect on what had been said to such an extent that when a second facilitator attempted a

	similar intervention the group were more responsive. They began to explore why the facilitator was saying this and more importantly how they could enhance their effectiveness. The group had begun to move forward.
Conclusion:	(i) You might not always see the immediate impact of your intervention, particularly whilst you are in the room as the group needs space to explore what has happened and become more reflective with each other (ii) The first intervention served to loosen the group, the second intervention enabled them to progress, proving that the value of series interventions (interventions which build upon each other) cannot be underestimated. (iii) Failure to achieve total success with your first intervention is not necessarily an indication of your shortcomings as a facilitator, as different groups respond to different styles, interventions and personalities of facilitator.

6

Facilitating Conflict

The term conflict tends to be associated with widespread unrest, mass forces and aggression. In the working context, conflict tends to be associated with head to head arguments and uninhibited expression of emotions. In reality conflict is far simpler; it is any occasion where there are divergent or opposing views. This does not have to result in outpourings of aggression to be conflict. It can easily be quite subtle, such as an idea being ignored, an alternative view being stated or individuals talking across each other. These situations do not necessarily result in disagreement, intense debate or a breakdown in the relationship but they do potentially serve to disrupt the smooth progress of conversation.

During this chapter we will explore how to facilitate when there is outright aggression but also the more subtle forms of conflict that emerge daily and serve to disrupt the working of teams.

Types of conflict

Traditionally conflict is regarded as a negative behaviour but in reality conflict brings discussion, debate, an alternative view and doesn't let issues pass superficially. This if channelled and managed well can serve to be a very positive source of stimulus. However negative conflict emerges from the failure to recognise and explore alternative perspectives and can often result in the breakdown of teams.

Positive conflict =   the proposal of alternative perspectives, resulting in debate, discussion and an enhanced result.

Negative conflict =   entrenched views and positions with little or nothing given either way, resulting in a standoff or the exertion of power by one party over another which leads to resentment and often retaliation, even if its delayed.

Most negative conflict situations grow surprisingly from potentially positive beginning, however the inclusion of emotion and intransigence can soon escalate the proceedings leading to the leap from positive to negative conflict.

Recognising conflict as a facilitator

The more extreme examples can be readily identified and range from outbursts, attacks and side swipes, yet the reality is that far too often conflict operates less overtly and this requires astute observational skills on the part of the facilitator.

The following observable examples are not intended to be exhaustive nor finite in identifying conflict, yet these in combination provide strong indicators of difficulty.

a) Individuals who initially contribute highly and then seem to withdraw from the conversation.

b) Individuals who seem to be constantly finding fault in others' proposals and arguments.

c) Non verbal behaviour such as quizzical looks, squirms and lack of eye contact.

d) Individuals who seem to focus on one or two members of the group to the detriment of others or rarely invite the contribution of some with the net effect that others are indirectly excluded.

e) Individuals persistently pressing the same point.

f) Patronising or condescending behaviour between group members.

Handling the conflict

In any of the above instances the key to successfully handling the situation rests with the ability to recognise the subtlety of the conflict. In many of these scenarios, merely raising the issues in a clear, non-judgmental manner serves to bring the issue to light and results in the raised item being discussed.

e.g. "I have noticed when an idea is raised, another idea is raised before the merits of the first idea are discussed." Rather than the loaded and judgmental response of: "nobody seems to be taking any notice of each other's ideas."

If for any reason these issues continue to be ignored, then increasing levels of confrontation should be applied by raising the fact that your intervention seems to have been ignored.

e.g. "Steve has raised an issue which seems to have been overlooked."

"To what extent is there merit in his idea?"

"I've mentioned Steve's ideas a couple of times but haven't had a response."

"I'm concerned that if we don't discuss this not only will an important issue be missed but we are likely to set a pattern that difficult issues are ignored."

Challenge & confrontation increases

In the instance of direct head to head conflict between 2 or more individuals where the typical behavioural responses are disagreement, finding fault in each other's arguments and pressing their own views, the role of the facilitator is to discourage the negativity and encourage the parties to focus on the areas of common ground rather than the differences. This serves to reduce the tension as well as focusing on what will work rather than what won't. Ironically as human beings we are often drawn to what we don't like in others' ideas or views rather than what we do like. By identifying the full range of positives, often a new solution can be generated which all can support.

e.g. "The danger at the moment is that we will end up in deadlock with neither of us prepared to move. I would suggest that we stop for a moment and identify what it is in others' views that we do agree with".

In both instances, the facilitator has encouraged the group to focus upon the issue at hand, rather than ignore it or allow it to build. This, coupled with a non-emotive style, one remaining calm and objective, is likely to move potentially emotionally charged situations into problem-solving scenarios.

The key principles of handling conflict

- Remain calm and non-emotional; the more you become heated, the more likely the conflict will escalate and even turn on you.

- Keep focused; don't allow yourself to be sidetracked from the source of the conflict. Often examples are thrown into the debate to illustrate points; these normally sidetrack the discussion as individuals delve into what and why this happened and find themselves defending their position.

- Remain neutral; it's essential that neither party perceives you as favouring one side over another. You may well internally agree with a particular view, however it is essential that this isn't shared.

- Review and reveal the thoughts, feelings, emotions and perspectives of each individual in order to regularly test out what conclusion they have now reached.

- Seek common ground by identifying what they do agree upon, no matter how narrow this is. Focusing upon the diversity of the views will only inflame the situation further.

- Stop the action and encourage each individual to reflect upon how their personal behaviour has contributed to the conflict, not what not what others did but what they have done. Typical responses are: "I'm not really listening" "I think I'm too entrenched". "I'm getting too worked up". "I'm only interested in what I've got say".

Skills Practice

1. There have been a number of debates in the group, but this intensifies and two individuals are at loggerheads over the way forward. What do you say and do?

2. One member of the group seems to cut across and discuss other's ideas whilst trying to railroad his own. What do you say and do?

3. The group seems to be making little progress; there are lots of ideas being put forward, but little response or action. What do you say and do?

4. The group is subdued and little is being said; you sense conflict but are unsure of the source, other than all are being guarded. What do you say and do?

5. Disagreements and dissatisfaction in the group is suddenly turned on you by one member, disgruntled at the progress being made. What do you say and do?

Suggested responses

1. Initially ask each of the individuals to identify what in their colleagues' proposal is of any interest or attraction. Collate the two sets of answers and begin to identify a third option which embraces the best of both offers. In addition before moving to this stage, ask each of them to identify what in their own behaviour is contributing to the difficulties. Encouraging each of them to share this will reduce any tension and also stimulate them to behave differently. Do not invite the pair to describe each other's behaviour as this will serve to intensify the problem.

2. There are a number of ways forward, from inviting others to comment, whilst asking the domineering individual to hold back, through to stopping the group and asking them each to describe their own and other's behaviour. Encouraging the group members to examine their own behaviour helps them to recognise how they are reinforcing the problem by not confronting the individual themselves. We would not suggest taking the individual head on as the facilitator, as the aggression may well be turned upon you and all the indications to date suggest that the group are unlikely to support you, thus you could become isolated.

3. Be direct, describe what you see happening and stop the group to explore these observations. Thereafter encourage the group to behave differently by stopping the action as incidents occur. As time goes by, others are likely to initiate these conversations themselves and so the group will begin to self-regulate.

4. As above, be direct and share what you see. If the group denies it, do not pursue the matter at that moment but watch to see how it unfolds. If you believe that the issue is continuing, either raise this again or discuss the matter, off line with individuals as a way of testing how much support you have, thereafter raise this once more, stressing the consequences of this behaviour .

5. Describe what has happened, be prepared to be open with the group, if you have contributed to the difficulties be honest with them and explain that it was not your intention. Then move onto describing the group's behaviour and ask them to consider what they are each contributing to the problem. Do not move on until there is agreement to resolve them.

7

Facilitation in Sport

The concept of sportsmen and women receiving coaching from experts is as established as the sports are themselves. Most Olympic athletes have their own personal coach whose role it is to dissect their performance and direct them towards the fine tuning which will create ultimate performance. All sports teams have at least one coach. Many have separate coaches for different elements depending upon the specialist skills and tactics being developed.

In all instances, the coach plays the role of analyser, dissector, guide and motivator. In effect, an expert is directing the individual forward. This is largely at odds with facilitation which is fundamentally concerned with helping others to do things for themselves and not creating dependency upon the facilitator.

My enthusiasm for both facilitation and sport first became entwined when I was introduced to a prominent Welsh rugby coach. He talked of his desire to resolve performance issues through team conversations. The reality was, however, that this tended to result in acrimonious arguments and ritual blaming of each other, with some very robust views being aired by some of the less articulate team members. Faced by these challenges, the coach's response was to go into battle with each of them and found himself embroiled in mayhem on more than one occasion. He was clear that he wanted them to take more responsibility for the team's performance, which meant greater ownership of both the problems and solutions, but he didn't know where to start.

We began by helping him to understand the role and objectives of a facilitator and he worked rigorously through a three day programme of skills acquisition. At times he talked of being out of his depth but then on other occasions he made quantum leaps in confidence. He left with a clearer picture of his role, what he was able to do and where he needed support.

We then sat down to examine how he structured his team conversations, which were, in effect, team reviews. What was evident was that there was no structure. He tended to ask a number of loose questions and within minutes, the conversation had either moved off on tangents or the team remained in silence, waiting for him to commence a monologue. As a result of our discussions, he decided to split his groups into the backs and forwards and prepared a set of key questions for each group. He then decided to facilitate the conversations separately. It was decided that he would handle these unsupported so that it seemed less like the latest gimmick to a group of fundamentally cynical rugby players.

Prior to entering into the discussion, we held a pre-meeting in order to establish his priority behaviours. During the meeting it was anticipated that he would need to ensure:

- Discussions didn't unduly wander and that he brought them back on track.

- Problems were raised but solutions not immediately sought in order that all team members had the opportunity to raise the issues as they saw them.

- Discussions were regularly summarised and agreements checked out with each individual.

- Practical ideas were generated and commitments made.

It transpired that the meetings started much like normal: jocular banter, a few skirmishes before silence and disinterest. Instead of embroiling himself in the skirmishes or responding to the silence with a monologue, the coach raised a number of searching questions, most of which hinged around the team's tactics and then left them to reach their own conclusions. Thirty-five minutes later, he returned to find the training methods had been rejigged, tactics questioned and realigned and enthusiasm and determination generated. The coach was amazed: months of hard effort had not achieved what had been accomplished in thirty-five minutes; and as the months passed... well it sounds like we're now leading to a happy ending where they won the league despite all odds.

This was far from reality. Their league position did improve, but not dramatically so. But what was inspiring was that this was achieved in the face of injuries to a number of key players and when inexperienced players were forced to stand in, the performance of the team continued. Why? Perhaps they were naturally good anyway, perhaps it was good fortune, perhaps the opposition was weaker. The coach believes that the team reviews generated commitment, determination, support and confidence with his players and thus in the absence of the key players, the substitutes readily stepped into the roles.

Over the last couple of years, I have become increasingly aware of the role that facilitation is starting to play in engendering commitment and ownership from team members. A former England manager on returning to manage a premiership side, let the players select the team for the first few weeks. Some might say this was anarchy, others saw this as a shrewd act from the manager. Each player picked his eleven, with the most popular selections becoming the team. In doing this, a number of tough decisions were confronted as the players were well aware of those team members who they felt were performing and equally those dragging their heels. What was the outcome? They were relegated! However, when the manager inherited the team they were 15 points adrift at the bottom, effectively already relegated. In the end, they missed out on staying up by 2 points.

Not everyone in the world of football is as willing to experiment. A colleague of mine described his brief association with a leading premiership club. Having been given permission to work with the team in encouraging them to review their performance, he duly conducted a day of reviews. The outcomes of the discussions and ideas for progressing were enthusiastically presented by the team to their manager. As he left, after what seemed a good day's work, the manager took the facilitator to one side and said; "Let's make a few things clear. They are paid to play. I am paid to think. Thank you and goodbye". At which point, what started as a promising venture, closed shut there and then. This does no more than reiterate the importance of engendering the manager's commitment, ownership and involvement in activities which directly affect his team.

Golfing Case Study

So far, my focus for facilitation in sport has been on team based activities; however, in Spring 1995, I was approached to work with a group of British women golfers. My experiences of working with them provided me with new insights and applications of facilitation. The remainder of this chapter describes this project.

Through my facilitation work in the business world, I was introduced to Mandy, a golfer working the European circuit. Mandy explained to me how she and four colleagues toured the European competitions together and had become increasingly aware of the level of support they could provide, despite competing against each other in the same tournament. It was with this far from meticulous brief that I ventured to a cottage deep in the heart of Surrey's stockbroker belt. As I entered the cottage, I was introduced to the other four golfers (who I shall refer to as Jane, Clare, Deborah and Lisa) and we sat down in the lounge to drink coffee.

During the ensuing two hours, we tried to establish some common ground as well as an agenda to work to, in a conversation which was punctuated with pars, birdies, and eagles. What became apparent was that I was faced by a mixture of cynicism, curiosity and enthusiasm, the latter primarily from Mandy. Eventually from the unstructured ponderings around the trials and tribulations of a golfer on the European circuit, we managed to identify five key areas for exploration.

Goal Setting

Individual

There was a need for clarity as to what each individual was trying to achieve, bearing in mind their differing levels of abilities, as well as different interests and agendas. One might have presumed that the objective of each player was to win the next tournament. True, that might have been their aim, but that was far from being the reality in such a highly competitive environment. Equally, their skills and abilities varied considerably; thus for each of them, financial survival was a prime consideration. For some, this was achieved through fees earned playing in Pro-am tournaments, where they would partner a leading businessman in return for a fee. For others they had managed to achieve a standing in the annual ratings which meant there was the possibility of some form of sponsorship; whilst occasionally their performance on the European circuit brought in the necessary capital.

Group

What could be realistically set as group goals? This initial discussion had certainly indicated that there was as much, if not more, uncommon ground as there was common ground. The relationships seemed fragile and fraught and infighting seemed to be frequent.

Pressures/Distractions

Golf is a strange sport, in that if you don't act, nothing happens. If you don't swing at the ball, the game stops. Nothing sensational here, other than that in every other sport, there is a stimulus which encourages the player to respond. In football, cricket, hockey etc, it's the opposition; in athletics, it's the sound of the gun, in field events a clock ticks by pressuring the competitor to act. Not in golf. The player could stand over the ball for days; OK those behind might become impatient, spectators may become bored, but unfortunately time allows many distractions and negative thoughts to enter the mind and so confidence, timing and belief can begin to become contaminated.

From our initial conversation, it became evident that each player was affected by totally different distractions and few had been able to overcome their particular Achilles heel.

Review

This seemed fundamental for them to progress together as a group, yet they had little or no idea of what it entailed and I barely knew how a concept so integral in the business world could be readily applied to five independent golfers. Nevertheless, there was something about it which seemed pertinent even if it meant establishing: when to review; how to review; and learning to handle each other on and off the course.

Understanding why we have an 8

Despite playing day in and day out and each player having their own dedicated coach who acts as their technical expert and advisor, each of the players failed to understand why they could play brilliantly in one tournament and collapse in the next. Conversation with their coaches reinforced their prescence, posture and swing at the ball but did little to address the saboteurs floating around in their heads. I certainly didn't see myself as some form of amateur psychologist or psychotherapist, but I did believe that a team of colleagues committed to supporting each other might find a way through the barriers.

Understanding each other

Beneath the disagreements and disputes which characterised the group lay a superficial understanding of both themselves and others. Any desire or intention to create support within the group would only come from a good understanding of each other's needs, strengths and limitations plus a willingness to overcome the differences.

The Outcomes

Goal Setting

We agreed to start our more detailed discussions by exploring individual and team goals. I asked each of them to spend sometime on their own mapping out what they saw as their personal goals, the priority goal for each of their colleagues as well as what the team could be like at its best, as well as at its worst.

We came back together and started with Clare, who saw her primary goal as winning a major tournament, secondly forcing her way into being one of the top 15 money names and thirdly securing a sponsorship deal. Each of the group in turn began to feed back to her, there was a remarkable amount of consistency; they each believed she had the potential to win a major tournament. What the goals lacked was a coherent plan for achievement.

We then began to dissect one of the goals and through working together create ways of getting there. The sponsorship deal was relatively easy to focus upon, we brainstormed who and why might someone be interested in sponsoring a high potential woman golfer. These ranged from institutions and businesses seeking to promote the role of women, to businesses seeking to break into new markets and without large amounts to spend. It then dawned upon them that in the mid 90's Daewoo were attempting to break into the car market with a strategy which appeared to be about getting as many cars on the road as possible. Clare sat down and mapped out her strategy and as a result of the conversation had identified six different options.

The team then turned to her goal of winning a major tournament; assessing how close she had come and what had interfered with this. Through this discussion it became apparent that the goal of winning a major tournament was too much of a long term goal in the context – so many interferences and without a coherent plan. When we studied the dilemma, to win a major tournament might require 190 steps (or 190 shots). Each step or shot would mean that the plan would need rewriting. For example, if Clare needed to score 3 on the first but scored four, the early holes would need to be studied and establish where this could be pulled back again. This process resulted in constantly thinking long term, building the pressure on the individual and consequently creating a greater degree of inconsistency so causing the pressures to mount even more. The desire to win a major tournament was nonetheless valid, however we decided that the goals needed to be more focused on the short term. If Clare focused on each hole at a time and sought to achieve the maximum score on each, thus ignoring her score on the previous holes or giving any thought to future holes then the pressure would recede, leaving her to relax and to play more naturally and consistently. This would serve to limit the escalation of the pressure and it would also mean a reduction in the endless calculations, particularly as her target score for the round may or may not be appropriate depending upon the performance of her competitors. If one was having a particularly good round she would need to constantly adjust her own targets.

Once we had made the quantum leap that goal setting should be hole by hole, the players became more focused and not distracted by their position in the tournament and ranking on the leader board. We were also able to map out the steps or shots for achieving success on each hole.

From now on a goal was a score on the hole, the achievement of that goal was to be achieved by a plan from tee to hole. This seemed rather straight forward, but when it's a matter of one's livelihood, the tournament interferences can soon riddle each player's thinking and thus concentration. The route to each hole became a new area for goal setting. From the discussion it became apparent that each player had different strengths and limitations – no surprises there – some were good at short putts, some long, some at driving or at chipping. Nothing radical here, other than as professional golfers I had expected that their skills and abilities would be relatively close. This was largely true, however in the professional world a marginal difference in one particular skill area could be the difference between a bunker, the rough or the hole itself. In essence, marginal differences exaggerated performance advantage.

The discussion established that the route to each hole needed to be a personal route, but much more significantly the decision for that route had largely been an individual activity, none of them were able to afford full time and rarely if ever part time caddies. This meant that no one was able to develop an intimate knowledge of their skills and abilities to be able to guide them. It was at this point the group came to the fore: over the years, each had begun to understand some of their fellow players' relative strengths and weaknesses and by accessing this data each player could make well informed decisions about their approach. We agreed to explore these issues in more depth even discussing reviews and a greater understanding each other.

Through the conversations with Clare, we had not only reached decisions which were pertinent to her, but had also set precedents for goal setting with each of the other players. By the end of the morning each player had their own personal plan for progress. At this stage, group goals had yet to be set, however as the conversations ensued, the common ground began to emerge and we decided to finalise the group goals at the end of the day. This also enabled any cynicism to be worked through during the session, thereby increasing the likelihood of engendering commitment to whatever the end goal might be.

Pressures/Distractions

In the initial two hours of exploration, the pressures and distractions during play reoccurred a number of times. All of the players found certain distractions significantly interfered with their performance and they were keen to generate ideas around each of their problems. So we headed into the arena, unsure of what we could achieve that their coaches had so far failed to do so. What transpired was a thorough conversation around each individual distraction, during which it emerged that these issues were rarely if ever broached by the individuals and certainly little attention was given to them by their coaches. The pressures/distractions are listed below together with the group's ideas for overcoming them.

Pressure/Distraction	Group Solutions
1. Rain/Wind On windy/rainy days Jane would tell herself "I'm not going to do well, my swing will be…"	• Deliberately practice when it's windy and raining. • During play, say to oneself: "what's the worst place this could go?" and then think "so what?" in the full knowledge that you know you can get out of that position, it's no longer a problem.
2. People Talking/Rattling Change Deborah found this distraction particularly difficult	• Walk away, do not continue to address the ball. • Take a sharp intake of breath to relax muscles. • Return to the ball and take very little

to handle as she was about to play a shot. It would wind her up and she would lose concentration.	time between addressing the ball and playing the shot in order not to lose concentration.
3. Slow Play Clare tended to be impatient and found slow play particularly frustrating and distracting.	• Between shots and holes write/read/talk to others. • This progressed to completing crosswords or playing pocket computer games whilst walking around.
4. Approaching a shot and thinking "I'm going to fat it" ? Lisa felt that at times she experienced crises of confidence: she would suddenly think "I am going to struggle with this shot"	• Pick a routine and stick to it, readdress the ball, two semi-swings and then strike the ball. • Don't change the routine, the more you change it, the stiffer and less relaxed your swing will be. • Work at your own pace.
5. Gamesmanship Clare had experienced little ploys by opponents during tournaments such as conversations which result in individuals being put down or distracted.	• Walk away. • Laugh – don't get drawn into the conversations. • Don't rise to the bait, nor give them the satisfaction of knowing that they've got to you.

6. Hit the ball badly in the practice area This affected all the players from time to time and as a result caused them to begin to worry and over-compensate their style before even setting foot on the course.	• Hit two good shots and then leave the practice area. • Don't hit more and more shots until you think you may get it right as it only increases the tension. • Don't practice – the previous weeks and months have been dedicated to it. This is similar to a student's approach to revising for exams: success comes from sustained long term effort, not from trying to cram five minutes before entering the exam room.
7. Freeze Jane raised the issue of approaching the ball and "freezing" – a major crisis of confidence which seems to have affected them all at some stage.	• Focus on a positive outcome; visualise the ball being swept off the turf. • Take a deep breath and let your shoulders drop, encouraging you to relax. • Walk away and come straight back to the shot, don't address the ball for more than 5 seconds.

The ease with which individuals talked of the inhibitions and at times their fears led us naturally into conversations about their own and others' strengths and limitations.

How could increased self-awareness help a professional golfer? They spent significant amounts of time together when away at tournaments.

Here behaviour not only affected their interpersonal relationships but for some of them profound effects on their performance. The group discussed how after a poor day on the course Deborah had joined them in the club rather than returning to the practice area in order to get it right. Unfortunately although the rest of the group realised that she should be in the practice area, not one individual confronted her, thus one poor day was followed by another. It transpired that Deborah knew she should have been practising but felt that she ought to join the others because she had committed to do so earlier in the day. More significantly she had strong needs to be liked and found it hard to say no. It was this type of incident that encouraged them to understand each other more thoroughly and through that identify ways to support each others performance.

Although the notion of exploring each other's strengths and limitations seemed conceptually apt, it was with much nervousness and trepidation that the process started. I initially suggested that they spent some time on their own considering themselves at their best, worst, as well as gathering their thoughts on their perceptions of their colleagues.

It was at this juncture I suggested that they split up and move to different parts of the cottage, not only to have some peace and quiet and enable them to concentrate, in reality to stop any nervousness or resistance percolating to each other. This would enable me to address any problems or issues individually rather than providing the group with a vehicle for collussion.

The conversation started with Clare. She began talking and at the earliest opportunity I invited the rest to respond and indicate whether her self perception matched their views of her. Despite the group's trepidation, they were remarkably candid and we were soon able to build up a picture of Clare. The challenge was to translate this increase self-awareness into action which could support and enhance performance on the golf course. What emerged was the real support each individual needed pre and post course activity, but since they were all playing in the tournament, it seemed there was very little they could do for each other. At best they may be partners for the round but it was more likely that they would be playing simultaneously but on another part of the course. Thus much of the ideas focussed upon reviewing as well as identifying means of encouraging and motivating each other.

Clare

At best		At worst	
• Happy	• Honest	• Can't communicate	• Affected by others, lets things get on top of her
• Laid back	• Challenging	• Unapproachable	
• Confident	• Keeps in contact with everyone		
• Sociable		• Bottles things up and keeps things to herself	• Goes quiet
• Independent	• Sensitive		• Independent
• When life is good is great to be with			• Sensitive
• Helps others to learn		• Makes it difficult for others to help	

Needs

- To get close to others but finds it hard.

- To tell people what she is thinking.

- For others not to be timid with her.

- For others not to hold back even is she gives the signs of wanting to be alone.

Deborah

At best	At worst
• Happy	• Worries about what people think
• Loyal	• Needs to be liked
• Giving/Generous	• Insecure
• Good Fun	• Avoids Confrontation Self-conscious
• Forgiving	• Lacks confidence
	• Sacrifices own needs to please others

Needs

• To have people around her.

• To be liked/recognised/respected.

• To feel valued and reassured.

• To be the centre of attention.

• For others to support and encourage her.

Jane

At best		At worst	
• Happy	• Trustworthy	• Stubborn	• Panics
• Sociable	• Loyal & Kind	• Doesn't Listen	• Let's small things niggle
• Honest	• Determined	• Easily Upset	
• Considerate	• Good Listener	• Paranoid	
• Organised		• Easily Influenced	
• Generous			

Needs

- To get help from others in terms of direction and support, particularly when she's panicking.

- To take her mind off golf; talk about other subjects to reduce her anxiety.

Mandy

At best		At worst	
• Generous	• Organised	• Sensitive, but hides it	• Independency gets in the way
• Helpful	• Talkative	• Stubborn	
• Great sense of humour	• Reliable	• Tends to take the lead	• Too hard on herself
• Happy	• Independent		
	• Leader	• Has to make her point	
• Relaxed		At times judgmental of others	
• Determined	• Doesn't care what people think		
• Kind			

Needs

• To have her own space at times.

• To also have people around her to talk to.

• To become lighter – less serious.

• To let go and enjoy herself when things aren't working out, rather than become sullen and worried.

Lisa

At best		At worst	
• Happy	• Helps others to learn	• Can't communicate	others to help
• Laid back			
	• Honest	• Unapproachable	• Affected by others, lets it get on top of her
• Confident			
	• Challenging		
• Sociable		• Bottles things up and keeps things to herself	
	• Keeps in contact with everyone		• Goes quiet
• Independent			
			• Independent
• When life is good is great to be with	• Sensitive		
		• Makes it difficult for	• Sensitive

Needs

- To have space on tour.

- To get closer to people but feels she can't trust them.

- To tell people what she is thinking.

- To have a laugh with the others.

- For others not to be afraid of her.

- For others not to hold back even if she gives signs of wanting to be alone.

Having established this level of understanding within the group, they were better positioned to provide real support for each other. During the feedback session, we stopped at regular intervals to review the progress towards our goal, but also the level of satisfaction. The review provided the forum in which we could really hone our approach. It also served as a source of motivation, as each player in turn was surprised, not by any new information given to them but more that their behaviours were so obvious to their colleagues. The insights also helped each of them to understand why frustration and friction occurred between them and served to encourage not only greater understanding but also increased tolerance.

So far the group had set personal goals, identified ways of overcoming pressures and distractions and encouraged a greater understanding of each other in order to provide support appropriate to each of their needs. What we needed to do was to develop a framework for supporting each other whilst competing in the tournaments: as a result, we set up the process of review.

Review

Reviewing during the tournament was going to be particularly difficult and reviewing during a round near impossible, as each of them was likely to be competing on a different part of the course at the same time, so it was agreed to review prior to the tournament and after the cut. In order to cause as little disturbance or curiousity with other players this was undertaken out of sight in a hotel room. To aid their approach during the review, the group developed their dos and don'ts in reviewing.

Do	Don't
• Talk about bad feelings and interferences. The review should be the forum in which barriers and blockages are discussed and overcome.	• Talk about specific problems you have or specific holes as this only serves to worry others about how to play that hole, despite the fact that they are likely to approach it very differently.
• Talk about how each of them overcame interferences, thereby sharing ways of maintaining concentration.	• Ignore success. When others are doing well encourage, celebrate and support. This will stimulate greater team support and it also reduces the degree to which others consume energy by worrying.
• Talk about the thoughts that went through your mind when playing a good shot, to encourage positive thinking.	• Get self-centred and upset; look for support
• Recognise that everyone will have played some good shots and inevitably some poorer shots. Try not to get a negative balance which could undermine confidence and thinking.	• Talk about what you were thinking before you hit a bad shot. It was felt that this would percolate to others and encourage them to have the same negative thought.
• Set short term goals which are not score related. From our experiences of goal setting we have learned that trying to get a certain score becomes too long term – even on a hole.	

Do (continued)	Don't (continued)
Thus the goals they began setting were more to do with their behaviour e.g. don't shuffle; two swings to address the ball; keep your head down for three seconds after hitting the ball.	

The day drew to a close and it became apparent that we couldn't deal with the whole agenda, so the issue of understanding 'why we have an eight' was put on hold for our next meeting. The next review was set for three weeks later, once they returned from the Austrian tournament.

Austrian Review

We met up three days after the tournament in a club house on a course in Oxfordshire. We sat around drinking coffee, laughing and chatting and gradually moved into the review. It transpired that initially things had gone to plan; they had each walked the course, studying the challenges and pitfalls. They had given thought to their own and others' game and come to the review meeting ready to thrash out their plans. Unfortunately although agreeing how each hole should be played; this failed to take into account each others' differing strengths and limitations. As a result, Clare and Jane, who were the most vociferous with their views, convinced the rest of the group to play safe. A fine strategy for them as they tended not to be big hitters but this didn't play to Mandy's strengths (she tends to be at her best when playing aggressively). They all played defensively and all scored higher scores than they might have expected on their first round.

The next night they adopted an alternative approach. They discussed the course arrangement individual by individual. Thus with the group's knowledge of each other they were able to advise each other accordingly. During our review, it had also become apparent that there was still some way to go to really understand the full extent of each others' golfing strengths and limitations. As a result the quality of advice each could give to each other was variable. Therefore it was agreed that in future they would vary who they practised with. This would also serve to push each others' standards higher, for example if the strong drivers always play with an underhitter then they tend to relax and feel comfortable with their game. However, when they meet individuals of equal ability this can come as something of a shock and affect their confidence. Equally underhitters can become demoralised if they constantly find themselves lagging behind.

As the review continued, it emerged that Deborah had entered the tournament unable to drive. She had become absorbed with this and spent every waking moment practising or becoming anxious. The group were all aware of this but didn't talk about it. Only at this meeting did they say she was over-reacting and she should concentrate on her pitching game. We delved into understanding why had they all stood back and watched rather than redirecting her and it became apparent that although they were becoming more confident in talking freely in this controlled environment, they had yet to make the transition to their everyday lives. They all made the commitment to say what they were thinking when they were thinking it in future; equally each of them would more readily ask for help and advice rather than thrash through their own problems on their own.

The conversation turned to the timing of the reviews with the group agreeing to undertake a planning meeting and then review just before the cut. This, however, proved to be inadequate because reviewing at the cut was somewhat too late for those who didn't make it. It helped them recognise where they had faltered and informed their approach in future tournaments but was too late for this competition. It was therefore agreed that the group should review at the end of the first day.

In addition to this learning, a member of the group talked about personal success. Although no one had won the tournament, they had never expected to; but what they did achieve were respectable placings as well as handling a number of difficult scenarios. Jane overcame a significant interference during play; Jane stopped and reviewed with Clare during play; and Mandy felt that she had some practical methods to aid her game.

Three weeks later the group set off for Denmark.

8

Facilitating Team Development

This chapter examines the process of facilitating teams, whether they are management, project or multi-functional teams. In particular, it explores the process of diagnosing and designing team events, which if inaccurately undertaken, will inevitably affect the facilitation of any team process. Much has been written about teams and groups and a variety of definitions offered.

In the context of this chapter, teams are defined as a group of individuals bound by common goals and some level of interdependence. Traditionally, many writers have differentiated teams as groups of individuals working towards a common goal. For many years, this has been upheld as a guide for teams; however increasingly with independent and isolatary working practices, individuals can be working towards a common goal, yet with little need if any, for contact or reliance on each other. The growth of flatter structures has resulted in managers and directors taking responsibility for the most disparate of functions. It is not uncommon for executives leading finance, IT and HR to report to the same director. Thus, common goals themselves are insufficient to bind teams together; individuals need to have some degree of interdependence to truly encourage teamworking. That interdependence manifests itself in some of the following resources, ideas, finance, support, working practices and the impact of decisions.

By contrast, groups are defined as individuals working towards a common goal but with no apparent need or level of interdependence. They may come together from time to time to share information or be briefed by the manager, yet they are wholly focused upon their own responsibilities, decisions made in one area have no impact on those in another. Much of the challenge for managers is determining whether they have a team or need to be a team or whether they are a group, superficially masquerading as a team. More often, some individuals seek and desire teamwork whilst others prefer to maintain group status.

For many managers, it is assumed that teams are the way forward and in many instances, this may be true, however, not all collections of individuals need to create teamwork and this is important to establish not least because of the amount of effort that creating great teamwork demands.

Diagnosis

Fundamental to the success of any team initiative is accurate diagnosis. It ensures that:

a. You have a clear understanding of the issues

b. You are prepared for the challenges ahead

c. You make the most appropriate decision on the most appropriate design

d. You build relationships with the team/group members

e. The participants develop their understanding of the issues

f. They are ready to embark on the process

g. They have the opportunity to air concerns and issues at the earliest opportunity

In approaching the diagnosis, there are a number of important recommendations.

1. Undertake your own diagnosis

It is important not to rely on others' diagnoses. I can remember inheriting a team project from a colleague who claimed to have undertaken some degree of diagnosis. Based upon this, I structured a four-day team event with senior Food Buyers, responsible for Food Strategy. On meeting the group for coffee shortly before the start of the event, it became very apparent that they saw no need for themselves to work as a team and were only really interested in their own areas of accountability. It transpired that the desire to enhance the quality of their teamworking had come from their line manager with little or no ownership from the individuals themselves. Needless to say, the design was quickly scrapped and a new approach hastily created which enabled them to explore and decide to what degree if any, they needed, wanted and should work together in the future.

Diagnosis is an art not a science, the way in which you hear and interpret issues will lead you to reach certain conclusions and thus inform your approach. Although in theory, all practitioners should reach the same conclusions, this is far from reality and it is unrealistic to think that personal bias and prejudices won't influence the design. What is important to recognise is the degree to which fact has influenced your approach rather than speculation and assumption.

2. Don't be trapped by dates for events

All too often, managers wanting to embark upon team development set the dates for an event and the diagnosis evolves around that. Withhold any commitment to an event until you are clear what the diagnosis is saying. In many instances, the manager is at the heart of the problem and they require one to one support and development, before any form of team gathering can be contemplated.

3. Define who the team is

This sounds all well and good and pretty much a statement of the blindingly obvious. With the complexity of management structures and working practices, what appears on paper rarely reflects the reality of how teams work. There are often many teams within teams, at times there are undeclared inner sanctums where the core decisions are made. It is important to get to the heart of these structures. In order that the team invention reflects the reality of the working practices not the theory of how it should be.

4. Once you've worked out who the team is, ensure you meet all of them

There is something about the law of teams, that if any one member is overlooked in the diagnostic phase, they become the thorn in your side. Either they have fundamental data that you either cannot access or foresee or their behaviour becomes difficult to manage.

In reality, the process of undertaking diagnosis is not a one-way process, true, it is an opportunity for you to gather essential data, but it is also the opportunity to build trust and credibility with all the team members. Furthermore, it enables you to begin to influence them in terms of the behaviour that is going to bring the optimum return for the team.

5. Manage the team leader's anxieties

Your confidential discussions with team members will inevitably induce paranoia within the team leader who at one level may be curious to learn what is being said or at another level, concerned. This does not mean letting yourself be drawn into revealing all the data that has been gathered, but more to be able to provide reassurance in preparing the leader for what is ahead. Through this process, one might recognise that the leader him/herself is at the core of the issues, in which case it may be that they need to undertake some preparatory work by equipping themselves with the skills to handle the challenges ahead. It is not uncommon for the starting point for team development to be one to one coaching for the team leader. This provides the team with the best possible opportunity for significantly moving forward.

THE TEAM DEVELOPMENT FRAMEWORK

In essence, there are 7 fundamental stages to team development and despite the variety of approaches adopted, they tend to fall into the following stages.

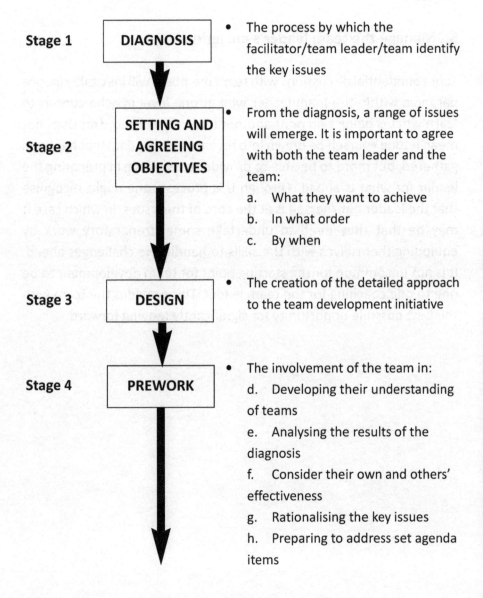

Stage 1 — DIAGNOSIS
- The process by which the facilitator/team leader/team identify the key issues

Stage 2 — SETTING AND AGREEING OBJECTIVES
- From the diagnosis, a range of issues will emerge. It is important to agree with both the team leader and the team:
  a. What they want to achieve
  b. In what order
  c. By when

Stage 3 — DESIGN
- The creation of the detailed approach to the team development initiative

Stage 4 — PREWORK
- The involvement of the team in:
  d. Developing their understanding of teams
  e. Analysing the results of the diagnosis
  f. Consider their own and others' effectiveness
  g. Rationalising the key issues
  h. Preparing to address set agenda items

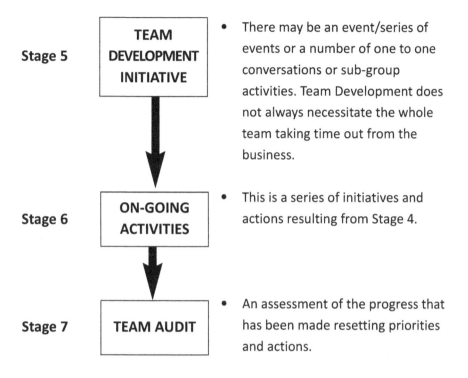

Stage 1 How do you Conduct Team Diagnosis?

In approaching the diagnostic phase of team events, there are 5 fundamental approaches that can be adopted.

i. Structured Interviews

A series of predetermined questions designed to elicit the strengths, limitations, problems and challenges both within and outside of the team.

ii. Group Discussion

The process by which members of the team are brought together to identify, discuss and clarify the issues.

iii. Diagnostic Inventories

A series of questions sometimes supported by rating scales designed to identify team members' perceptions of both the team's effectiveness and issues and challenges within it.

iv. Psychometric Testing

The use of a battery of psychometric tests can provide invaluable insight into the relative strengths and limitations of each team member. By subsequently analysing the commonalties, trends and variations, this can provide some indicators of likely team behaviour and potential.

v. Diagnosis during the Event

Using the event itself as the forum for diagnosing the issues.

Structured Interviews

Strengths	Limitations
• Consistent in approach	• Time consuming and often difficult to set up in advance
• Provide opportunities for information to be clarified	• If adopted rigidly, doesn't cater for variations or issues not anticipated
• Provides opportunities for the facilitator to build relationships and particularly trust with the team	• Can be perceived as threatening by the team members
• The structure allows comparisons of the data to be made	• Relies on the facilitator's ability to draw out the data
• Allows misapprehensions and concerns to be addressed	

Group Discussions

Strengths	Limitations
• Allows issues to be debated, clarified and the real problems and concerns to be identified	• If not managed well, the facilitator can find themselves actually conducting the team event there and then without all team members being present
• Can encourage the team development process to start before the event itself	• Can be difficult to set up with team members' conflicting diary arrangements
• Allows concerns and misapprehensions about the team event to be resolved	• Team members may be reluctant to discuss the real issues in front of and with their colleagues

Diagnostic Inventories

Strengths	Limitations
• Standardised approach encourages comparisons to be made of the data • Relatively risk free method that can encourage individuals to state their thoughts with few inhibitions • Can be administered relatively quickly and requires little facilitator time • Provides an opportunity for clarification of issues	• Can cause more confusion than clarification as individuals often don't provide the reasoning for their decisions • Individuals often regard it as another job to do on their mounting list of priorities and so can easily be discarded • No team inventory can fully capture every possible facet within teams without being such a daunting document that it undermines team members' desire to complete it

Psychometric Testing

Strengths	Limitations
• Objective and dispassionate analysis • Provides invaluable insights into the individual's strengths, weaknesses and potential • Can be completed at the team members' convenience • The feedback process can serve to encourage the team members to approach the event in the most receptive manner	• Provides insight into the individuals, however, will not provide a comprehensive view of the team issues • Team members can find the intrusions intimidating • Requires significant amount of the facilitator's time for analysis • Requires planning and commitment to ensure adequate time for the completion of the test, the analysis of the results and the feedback process

Diagnosis during the Event

Strengths	Limitations
• Requires less time and preparation in advance of the event • Provides opportunities for all to become involved in identifying the issues • Enables events to be set up very quickly	• The facilitator cannot be sure of what is ahead for them as they have no insights into the team's effectiveness • Individuals may be less likely to express their true views on issues in front of their colleagues • More challenging for the facilitator to build relationships with the team members as they balance the need to build trust, with establishing the true issues and challenging views and opinions

Structured Interview Questionnaire

Introduction

- Purpose of the interview
- My background
- Their background
- Climate of conversation

Areas for Exploration

Team Direction

- Purpose of the team
- Vision
- Strategy
- Objectives

Relationships with other teams

- Boundaries and parameters of operation
- Strengths/weaknesses of relationship
- Inter-relationships and interdependencies

Team Dynamics

- Behaviours
- Rules of operation
- Inter-relationships – strengths/limitations
- Meetings – frequency, duration and purpose

Team Members

- Their roles
- Performance of individuals
- Relative strengths, weaknesses, contributions and impact
- Relationships with others

Summary of the Key Themes

HOW DO YOU FEEL ABOUT TEAMWORKING?

The 10 questions below are designed to assess your attitude towards various aspects of teamworking and to stimulate your thinking and group discussion about them. There are obviously no 'right' or 'wrong' answers to the questions below. Therefore, please check each item as you see it.

For each item below, circle the **one** number, which best represents how you feel about it.

	Strongly Disagree	Disagree	Undecided	Agree	Strongly Agree
1. Teamwork proceeds best when all team members speak freely or level with each other as opposed to hiding opinions or feelings	1	2	3	4	5
2. An effective team faces up to and encourages disagreements as opposed to smothering differences	1	2	3	4	5
3. Strong feelings, including anger, if expressed will aid teamwork in the long run	1	2	3	4	5
4. It is important that decisions be made by talking things through – achieving consensus – rather than voting or merely relying on a decision by the boss	1	2	3	4	5

	Strongly Disagree	Disagree	Undecided	Agree	Strongly Agree
5. An effective team gives support, recognition, encouragement and earned praise to group members easily and freely	1	2	3	4	5
6. Silent members should be drawn into discussions so that the ideas of everyone are secured and no-one feels left out	1	2	3	4	5
7. It is important that teamwork contributes to all members feeling good about themselves and one another	1	2	3	4	5
8. Leadership roles (eg initiating, clarifying, summarising) should be shared among the team so that all members develop from the group work experience	1	2	3	4	5
9. 'Feedback' to team members should be freely given so that people will know when they are helping or hindering the group's progress	1	2	3	4	5
10. An effective team should stop the action now and then and evaluate its own functioning	1	2	3	4	5

EXAMPLE OF 360° QUESTIONAIRE

Name of Manager: _____

Instructions to Team Members

Your manager is shortly to attend a Leadership Development Programme, aimed at helping them to be thoughtful about their personal performance and that of the team that they lead. Part of the programme will be aimed at giving them accurate information about the views of team members, to enable practice to be compared with theory.

You are asked to assist with this process by completing the following 2 questionnaires entitled:

Team Effectiveness Review

Team Leader Assessment

The questionnaires will be analysed, in confidence, by the consultant running the programme and the overall results of all respondents fed back to your manager on the programme itself.

You are not asked to include your name on the questionnaires, so that you can concentrate on your personal assessment. Please be as honest as possible. Please ensure, however, that your manager's name is included.

Please return your questionnaires by:_____

Part One

Team Effectiveness Review

The way in which a team operates can simply be the result of the working practices that evolve over time, ie teamwork habits can develop with little or no conscious effort on the part of the team leader or its members. Even where the leader tries to establish a positive teamwork culture, he or she may find their intentions in open or covert conflict with the needs or expectations of team members. Further, a team leader's attention will be devoted to the things they know/understand/believe to be important and will therefore be limited by their training or experience.

As a result, it is important to take stock of a team's effectiveness from time to time, as it is not unusual for everyday work practices to differ from the intentions of the team leader and the individual members. Despite good intentions, everyday work pressures can conspire to detract from good teamwork, and for many reasons, **actual** practices often differ from the **ideal**.

This questionnaire has been written to identify where such differences exist in your team. For each heading, you are given 5 examples of how the team might deal with the issue. From these you are asked to indicate which alternative is closest to your belief of what **ideal** teamwork would be like. You are asked to indicate which of the alternatives is closest to the **actual** practice within your team. Should none of the alternatives prove suitable, you have the option of entering your own statement. Where your **ideal** and **actual** answers differ, you are asked to cite a couple of obvious examples to substantiate your view.

1. Within this team, teamwork is seen as:

Ideal   **Actual**

1. Something which happens when we all have to pull together in the face of adversity, otherwise we are left to our own devices

2. Unnecessary; people are given the space and freedom to channel their energies and creativity into their work. People are treated as adults and trusted to get on with their work

3. The basis for creating a harmonious and friendly environment where individuals enjoy working together. Mutual support and encouragement are used to get the best out of people

4. Something to which only lip service is paid. All the right words are said but working practices and time pressures make a nonsense of teamwork

5. The basis for ensuring everyone operates in a dynamic and commercial way. People are committed to acting in a way which enhances the team's reputation and credibility

Examples that support my actual choice are:

_____

_____

_____

2. Planning, monitoring and feedback are seen as:

Ideal   **Actual**

1. [ ]   [ ]   Theoretical concepts which we should be doing, but which the pressures of work make impossible. We tend to rely instead on "keeping our fingers on the pulse" or relying on intuition

2. [ ]   [ ]   Informal activities which are carried out in a way that best fits in with the team leader's needs or availability

3. [ ]   [ ]   A means of keeping everyone involved and informed. They are used to ensure discussions are carried out in a way which praises people's efforts and generally raises morale

4. [ ]   [ ]   Essential management activities. Team members treat these activities as priorities, making time to ensure that individual and collective activities are well planned and implemented

5. [ ]   [ ]   The best way of keeping work activities carefully controlled

Examples that support my actual choice are:

_____

_____

_____

3. Teamwork on a day to day basis is:

Ideal　　　　**Actual**

1.
Non-existent; the way we are structured/operate means that there is no basis for teamwork. We are given the scope to operate as individuals; teamwork is something that occurs elsewhere in the organisation

2.
An example to the rest of the organisation. We continually review our effectiveness, challenge and support each individual's contribution and work together to ensure that decisions are effective and accepted by all

3.
Demonstrated by the fun, enjoyment and stimulation we all experience working together. We might not find time to discuss all the important issues, but our morale is high and we enjoy working together

4.
Infrequent and quite formal. We tend to operate as a large committee, with contentious issues rarely discussed in depth. All the real decisions are taken outside of the team

5.
Dominated by the team leader's influence. Other individuals do not assert themselves. Often we pay lip service to what the leader wants or conform to his/her expectations on important issues

Examples that support my actual choice are:

_____

_____

_____

4. Decision making is something which:

Ideal   **Actual**

1. Occurs on an expedient basis. We seem to take one decision during a team meeting, only to decide to do something else when we meet again. We lack consistency in the way we tackle things

2. Seems to be limited to those issues where there is no conflict between team members. As a result, we seem to steer clear of important but contentious issues

3. Largely reflects what the team leader and one or two vociferous members of the team want. Alternative views are either not listened to, or worse still, not even expressed

4. Is left to each individual's professional judgement. We recognise the experience and talent of individuals and expect them to manage their own responsibilities

5. Is based on a careful analysis of all facts. Full contribution is encouraged and decisions are only made after full and informed debate. Once made, the decision receives the full commitment and backing of the whole team

Examples that support my actual choice are:

_____

_____

_____

5. Within this team we see mutual trust and support as:

Ideal   **Actual**

1. Something which only occurs when we come under attack from those outside the team. We stand together in the face of criticism or conflict, defending individual decisions through collective action

2. Typified by the loyal and professional way individuals act as representatives of the team. They conscientiously carry out their personal commitments following a team decision

3. Non-existent. Everyone goes their own way and stands or falls by their own efforts

4. Essential to individual and collective achievement. The team offers encouragement and help to individuals so that they do not fail to achieve what is required of them

5. Something which is based on circumstance. We trust individuals to deliver, but are prepared to discuss how to support them when they ask

Examples that support my actual choice are:

_____

_____

_____

6. Communications within the team occur on the basis that:

	Ideal	Actual

1. □ □ It is up to the team leader to keep everyone up to date and that he/she should structure meetings to elicit the information they need

2. □ □ People are told only what their colleagues feel they need to know. Conversations are kept to what has been done and what has to be done rather than examining the way in which things happen

3. □ □ Effective teamwork is based on a climate of openness and honesty where people speak freely about any issue in the team

4. □ □ Team members are somewhat wary of one another and tend to be polite and professional in the way they say things, wishing to avoid controversy or criticism

5. □ □ Whoever talks longest/loudest wins. Our competitive culture spills over into our communications with one another, with all conversations seen on a win:lose basis

Examples that support my actual choice are:

_____

_____

_____

7. In this team we handle conflict by:

	Ideal	Actual	
1.			Seeing it as the basis of creative/ effective problem solving
2.			Seeking compromise solutions
3.			Leaving it to the team leader to decide
4.			Suppressing it
5.			Accentuating the positive and trying to reduce inter-personal difficulties

Examples that support my actual choice are:

_____

_____

_____

_____

_____

_____

8. We tend to view innovation as:

Ideal   **Actual**

1. [ ]   [ ]   Something which we are not expected to do. We respond/react to changes which are initiated elsewhere in the organisation

2. [ ]   [ ]   One of the important by-products of effective teamwork, where the combined efforts of the team ensure existing methods are challenged and new options are identified and implemented

3. [ ]   [ ]   Something best left to an individual's technical judgement. The team will comment on ideas if required but the individual has the ultimate responsibility

4. [ ]   [ ]   A potential source of conflict and we tend to channel our efforts into refining and improving existing methods rather than disrupting things by constantly changing them

5. [ ]   [ ]   Something we talk about but rarely do

Examples that support my actual choice are:

_____

_____

_____

9. This team tends to use established procedures to:

Ideal   **Actual**

1. [ ] [ ] Provide the basis of order and predictability. There are unwritten rules which govern the way we operate and we all prefer this uniformity and consistency

2. [ ] [ ] Cut off conflict, using precedent to guide decisions if no clear answers seem likely to emerge quickly

3. [ ] [ ] Reinforce and sustain itself. We enjoy the rituals and habits we have developed to reinforce our feelings of belonging

4. [ ] [ ] Stimulate the need for change. There is a fear of complacency that encourages us to push for different and better ways of doing things

5. [ ] [ ] Act as a means of ensuring that individual responsibilities are met. They provide the basis for keeping people on track and productive

Examples that support my actual choice are:

_____

_____

_____

10. We tend to view team reviews as:

(In this context, a review is a rigorous discussion of the pros and cons, strengths and weaknesses areas for development. It should not be confused with a range review, which is an examination of proposed goods)

	Ideal	**Actual**	
1.			An opportunity for celebration and congratulation. We are good at praising one another and have developed effective techniques for keeping our morale high
2.			A bit unnecessary. By the time we get around to reviewing things, we see forthcoming tasks as priorities and consequently minimise the amount of time we spend living in the past
3.			An opportunity to ensure we consolidate our learning from experience. We analyse issues fully and try to strike a good balance between reviewing successes and failure. Our reviews help us to keep our teamwork right
4.			Something to be used for analysing the unexpected. We tend only to review those issues which caught us unprepared or when things did not go according to plan
5.			Important in diagnosing why things went wrong. We are quick to spot flaws and omissions and channel our efforts into fault-finding with a view to avoiding making the same mistakes twice

Examples that support my actual choice are:

_____

_____

Part Two

Team Leader Assessment

1. What aspects of your team leader's behaviour do you see as most positive and constructive in terms of getting the best out of the team, either individually or collectively?

2. What improvements would you like to see in your team leader's performance, ie what modification/changes would help enhance their effectiveness?

3. How would you rate the leadership qualities of your team leader?

POOR	INADEQUATE	OK	GOOD	OUTSTANDING

Briefly explain your choice.

4. Do you see your team leader as oriented/committed to building and developing an effective team? YES/NO

Why?

Stage 2   Setting and Agreeing the Objectives

There is very little point in embarking upon any team development initiative, without clarity as to the purpose and the specific objectives to be achieved. To reach this stage, it is suggested that the facilitator analyses and summarises the key themes emerging from the diagnosis ensuring that there is some sense of balance to the positives and negatives of the team. Armed with this data, discussions should be held with at least the team leader, but ideally the whole team in order to convey the key messages and secure their commitment to the next stage.

Stage 2 is essential in alleviating two fundamental challenges:

1. Prioritising the vast array of issues into objectives for the ensuing phases.

2. Encouraging the ownership of the data to move from the facilitator to the team itself.

Typical team development objectives are:

- To create a vision and strategy for x, y, z functions

- To identify the strengths and limitations of our current working practices

- To identify the strengths and limitations of our own personal effectiveness

- To set the roles, responsibilities and accountabilities of each team member

- To develop a plan for achieving a, b, c.

Stage 3   Designing the Team Event

Having undertaken the diagnosis, consolidated and analysed the data, the next stage is to design the team event. If this is to mean time taken out off-the-job, the amount and specific dates need to be agreed at this stage. This allows the facilitator to determine not just the design of the off-the-job element, but the nature and amount of prework to be undertaken thereby maximising the time when the group are together. In reality, the more that can be achieved either through analysing the issues, or developing the participants' understanding of themselves, others or teams the greater the amount of progress that can be achieved during the event.

Many practitioners would assert that one should design the event first and then guide, encourage or at times cajole the team leader to make the commitment to meet these requirements. However, the realities of the commercial world rarely coincide with the ideals of practitioners and thus the two can often collide. I am certainly not suggesting that once the team leader states what they are prepared to offer that this is not challenged, the constraints examined and if this is barely enough to scratch the surface, then you can't extract yourself from this team development initiative. More, I am proposing that the facilitator starts with the realities and practicalities and ensures this is realistic enough to meet the objectives.

Once the timescales have been set, the facilitator can begin to create the learning framework and then determine the necessary amount of prework.

What follows, are two examples of team development designs.

> # A two day event for an intact team, ie a team leader and his/her direct reports

Objectives

1. To identify the strengths and weaknesses of current working practices
2. To agree a plan for furthering the team's performance

Day 1

09.00 Introductions and team event purpose
09.45 Working in subgroups, analysing the diagnostic report and prioritise the issues
12.30 Lunch
13.30 Present the priority issues to the whole group
15.00 Whole group reaches consensus on the prioritised issues
16.30 Subgroups produce recommendations for addressing the issues, continued overnight until mid-morning

Day 2

10.30 Whole group agrees recommendations
14.00 Action plan developed, names and commitments agreed
17.30 Close

A one and a half-day event for a new project team

Objectives

1. To agree the terms of reference of the project team
2. To understand and be able to positively exploit team members' strengths and minimise the impact of their weaknesses
3. To agree the project team's working practices
4. To agree a project plan

Day 1

12.30 Introductions and project terms of reference by project sponsor

14.00 Presentations by each individual highlighting their own strengths and limitations based upon their prework

17.00 Brainstorm of the behaviours, attitudes and working practices of project teams that have worked well and those that have been ineffective

Day 2

08.30 Agreeing behaviours, attitudes and working practices of this team, including the roles, responsibilities and expectations of each other, the frequency and purpose of meetings, the tone and climate of those meetings

14.00 Producing the project plan
Closure on production of final plan

9

The Top Tens

Top 10 excuses at 3/6 month reviews for not doing anything

- I've been away on courses
- I've changed jobs
- I'm involved in a new project
- The time didn't seem right
- I've lost my action plan
- Fred was going to contact me, but he's been busy and I've been busy, we've tried to meet but …
- I haven't had time
- I wanted to give some thought to it all
- My boss has changed, so I wanted to let him settle in
- I thought I'd use today as a way of getting my thoughts together

Top 10 defensive statements

- I'm not like that at work
- You don't know me as my people do
- They've misinterpreted the questions, what they mean is …
- My manager likes me to be like that
- That's how they expect to be treated
- I've always been like that and it doesn't seem to have stopped me
- My people always find it hard to fill in these questionnaires that way, either:

    a. some statements have been left off, or

    b. there are different perceptions, or

    c. some questionnaires haven't been returned

- You don't understand my environment – it works
- You have to be like that to work where I do
- I'm not normally like this it's because of the course

Top 10 worst interventions during conflict in the group

- Anyone for a cup of tea?
- It's funny how these things turn out well in the end
- Who started it?
- I think you'd better go outside and sort it out
- Have some plasters
- I'll be back later when you're a lot happier
- Are you enjoying the process?
- Learning a lot?
- Calm down, let's not take these things too seriously, it's only a course after all
- Whose fault is it?

Top 10 excuses:
Is that really the problem?

- It's just before lunch, just after lunch, last thing of the day, start of the day

- It's because we didn't change the group

- We weren't briefed properly

- The handouts weren't clear

- The group confused me

- We didn't have enough time

- The room was too hot/cold, too large/small, too light/dark

- It's because we're a new group

- We've tried

- We got it right, the rest got it wrong

Top 10 all time great rationalisations by groups for why they achieved less than they could

- It's early in the morning, we've just warmed up
- It's the graveyard session
- It's lunchtime, dinner, tea
- It's only a course; management exercise
- It's not the real world
- We could have achieved more if we'd wanted to, but weren't motivated
- It doesn't really matter
- You didn't brief it properly
- We're never good at games, but if it's work, that's different
- We wouldn't normally be like this

Top 10 ways of retaining sanity when facilitating

- Tell yourself that you are there to help, but if they don't want help, it's their problem

- Your perceptions and feelings are valid no matter how much they deny this

- They are always part of the problem if not all of it

- You can only be as good as the group you're working with

- Reassure yourself, it's good to live in the distain of the group, it shows you are stretching the range of your interventions

- They do like you really and will at some time see the light and appreciate why you are doing what you are doing

- Have another go

- Let someone else have a go

- Go to another group

- It's the group processes at fault not your facilitation, it's just they haven't found out how to make good use of you yet

Top 10 myths about icebreakers

- No course can work properly without an icebreaker
- Icebreakers put people at ease – they merely delay the inevitable
- There's no better way of breaking down barriers than using icebreakers
- Throwing balls at each other and naming who you are throwing them to, develops relationships as well as manual dexterity skills
- A good trainer needs a range of icebreakers to cover every eventuality
- Icebreakers are time effective as they allow individuals to expend energy on the programme rather than go off to the gym
- When it comes to those sticky moments on a programme, call on an icebreaker
- Discomfort, uncertainty and worry at the start of the programme is overcome by icebreakers
- Good icebreakers are a great way to create a relaxed atmosphere – but so is a free bar
- Icebreakers create high energy

In reality, icebreakers do no more than distract the group from the source of the issue. If a group is low on energy, running around may raise their energy levels whilst they are outside, but will do little for their group behaviour, once they return to the syndicate room. The issue of low energy needs to be addressed directly rather than delayed by undertaking superficial activities. At the start of the programme, individuals are likely to be anxious and worried about what lies ahead, delaying dealing with this directly by introducing icebreakers merely seems to heighten worries.

Top 10 ways to establish your credibility as a facilitator

- Name as many chief executives and top companies you work in without drawing breath

- Always have a model for any occasion which no-one has either heard of or is interested in

- Cover up any regional accent and develop a verbose Home Counties dialect

- Make sure your first intervention is so long and ponderous that you can sit back for the rest of the programme

- Always have an example of how you successfully handled that same situation ideally many years ago

- Make sure you wear a badge saying 'Facilitator' and ensure all your participants wear badges marked 'Delegate'

- Don't do any menial tasks, like coffee or room layouts – delegate it to your co-facilitator

- In delegating tasks to your co-facilitator, make sure you have an audience in so doing

- Stay on your feet at all times, but ensure your delegates remain seated

- In delivering methodologies, pause for effect

Top 10 misconceptions groups have of facilitators

- Every facilitator needs a manual
- That you will tend to their every need, bring tea and coffee to them at their beck and call
- When things don't work out, that you should have done something about it
- That you have an intimate knowledge of every aspect of their business, particularly abbreviations and shorthand
- That you know every management theory going
- That you naturally enjoy reading books
- That the entrances and exits of facilitators into rooms has deep and meaningful reasons rather than the result of mild curiosity
- You are a psychologist and study their every move
- That you spend your weekends analysing your family's behaviour
- That inactivity is a sign of reflection rather than confusion and boredom

Top 10 essential tools for a facilitator

- Use flipcharts to make planned presentations seem like you've done it spontaneously
- Blu-tack – the ultimate height of trainer technology
- Have the largest desk in the room, at the front with the essentials for drawing attention to yourself, a water jug with adorning bottles of orange, lime and blackcurrant, plus at least 3 glasses
- Marker pens; red, blue, green and black for junior facilitators, a full selection for established/ senior facilitators
- 2 packs of lined paper, sparingly used
- A pair of white training shoes for that quick intervention
- A pack of pencils, but obviously no pencil sharpener
- A two hole punch for those four hole punch moments
- A cardigan, cords and sandals (summer only)
- A wealth of handouts so that delegates feel they are getting value for money

---

Top 10 key behaviours of a facilitator

- If you are not sure of something, put the issue back to the group

- When you are sure, take a tortuous route of questioning until eventually the group come up with your answer for themselves

- Always maintain a knowing look on your face, it will lead groups to think there's more in your head than there actually is

- If you are asked a direct question, look away and hope someone else answers

- Constantly check upon your colleague with the briefing they have given, it builds trust

- To get the group's attention, use increasing levels of coughing

- When sub-discussions break out within groups, try using phases like:
  "One meeting please"
  "I think some points are being missed"
  "I don't think we are listening as well as we could do"

- Make sure that when asking questions, you target them at individuals, this will keep them on their toes, allow others to relax and not encourage them to usurp your power

- If time is running out, suggest that the group talk about it in the bar tonight, in the full knowledge that by then, no-one will be slightly interested in the debate

- At times of conflict and uncertainty, always have a witty anecdote to draw upon, it tends to lighten the atmosphere

Top 10 excuses for not reviewing

- It's too early
- We're too tired
- I can't think of anything
- It's the facilitator's responsibility
- I can't think of any negatives
- There's no point in saying things for the sake of it
- If it ain't broke don't fix it
- Reviews are for problems
- Reviewing will make us worse
- We haven't got time, there are too many things to do